PRAISE FOR
GOODBYE, HURT & PAIN

"This is so much more than a book! It's an insightful guide to experiencing greater freedom, ease, and success. I've had profound experiences with RIM and this book exceeded my expectations. Get a copy for yourself and someone you love. You'll be glad you did!"

— MARILYN SUTTLE, author of *Who's Your Gladys? How to Turn Even Your Most Difficult Customer into Your Biggest Fan*

"Ground breaking and innovative, best-selling author Dr. Deborah Sandella provides a sacred road map to bypass logic and get to the heart of lingering pain. Using leading-edge research and techniques to shift your body's experience, you'll ultimately transcend even the most painful experiences and discover your innate ability to forgive and love. I highly recommend."

— DR. SHAWNE DUPERON, six-time Emmy® winner, founder of Project Forgive

"With her book *Goodbye, Hurt & Pain*, Dr. Deborah Sandella makes the case for how we can rapidly activate deep, lasting healing. I recommend it."

— BARNET BAIN, director of *Milton's Secret*, producer of *What Dreams May Come*, author of *The Book of Doing and Being: Rediscovering Creativity in Life, Love and Work*

"In her new book *Goodbye, Hurt & Pain*, Dr. Deborah Sandella offers life-changing steps to a better life. It's a must-read!"

—SHERI FINK, inspirational speaker and author

"If you want to live the most inspired life possible, you will need to deal with your amazing emotions. And Deb Sandella provides a groundbreaking, magical, and credible approach to instantaneously shifting our feelings. Mark this day—because this is a powerful process you're going to use again and again."

—TAMA KIEVES, *USA Today* featured visionary career catalyst and best-selling author of *A Year without Fear: 365 Days of Magnificence*

"Dr. Deborah Sandella is changing the way we perceive our emotional selves. Her book *Goodbye, Hurt & Pain* shows us that we have a smart emotional operating system with greater resourcefulness and adaptability than we've ever thought. This book is uplifting and inspiring."

—MARCI SHIMOFF, #1 *New York Times* best-selling author, of *Happy for No Reason*

"Dr. Deborah has found a way to share information on techniques for transforming challenging emotions into life-affirming expression. Take a dive into this work, commit to your growth and then expect miracles."

—CYNTHIA JAMES, international author/teacher and author of *I Choose Me: The Art of Being a Phenomenally Successful Woman at Home and at Work*

"What Steven Covey is to living a highly successful life, Dr. Deb is to health, love and success. *Goodbye, Hurt & Pain* offers a brilliant combination of engaging reading with understandable neuroscience."

—TERESA DE GROSBOIS, #1 international best-selling author of *Mass Influence*

"Dr. Deborah Sandella in her book *Goodbye, Hurt & Pain* offers us a user-friendly guide to an easier and less stressful way of living. We all want that! I have learned much from working with Dr. Deb and have used her work in many settings—even with my corporate clients. This book gives you access to Dr. Deb's deep wisdom and is presented like a warm, personal chat that left me feeling excited and inspired. I highly recommend that you buy this book and put it into practice right away!"

—PETE WINIARSKI, best-selling author, business transformation expert, and CEO of Win Enterprises, LLC

"Dr. Sandella's *Goodbye, Hurt & Pain* is a practical, down-to-earth method of realizing the immense potential that lies within everyone. She is a skillful guide who writes from experience and with gentle compassion."

—LARRY DOSSEY, MD, author of *ONE MIND: How Our Individual Mind Is Part of a Greater Consciousness and Why It Matters*

"*Goodbye, Hurt & Pain* makes sense! Dr. Deborah Sandella's empowering steps to create a healthy flow of feelings is transformative and surprisingly easy and enjoyable. Her proven system for removing unconscious blocks frees us to use conscious desire to attract the life we're meant to live."

—CATHY AND GARY HAWK, award-winning authors of *Get Clarity: The Lights-On Guide to Manifesting Success in Life and Work.*

"If you have ever wanted to develop your inner life, hone your intuition or connect with the healer within, Deborah Sandella makes it easy and delightful. Her RIM meditations are a masterful guide that can help uncover the core of peace, creativity, compassion, and delight that resides within you."

—JOAN BORYSENKO, PHD, author of *The PlantPlus Diet Solution: Personalized Nutrition for Life* and *Minding the Body, Mending the Mind*

"This book has the potential to change your life in amazing ways. *Goodbye, Hurt & Pain* is a user-friendly guide to better moods, relationships, and results. Dive in and enjoy the transformation!"

—ELLEN ROGIN, CPA, CFP(R), co-author of the *New York Times* best-selling *Picture Your Prosperity*.

"Dr. Deb shares a new technique that transforms anxiety, worry, and fear into confidence, joy, and success. *Goodbye, Hurt and Pain* is filled with exercises and inspiring examples that give us a fresh and profound approach to creating health, love, and fulfillment that is nothing short of miraculous. Highly recommended!"

—PEGGY CAPPY, creator of *Yoga for the Rest of Us* as seen on public TV

"Each generation must rediscover and reframe for itself how our emotions rule us unless we understand them. Dr. Sandella's practical, good sense does splendidly for a new generation. She shares sound advice and a wealth of experience with real people."

—ROBERT FREEDMAN, MD, Professor of Psychiatry, University of Colorado, and editor of the *American Journal of Psychiatry*

For anyone who feels stuck, unfulfilled, or just knows there can be more to life than you're now experiencing, this is the book can help open an exciting way of experiencing yourself and the world around you. If life is a stage, Deb Sandella would receive a standing ovation for one of the most liberating books of our time. Bravo, Dr. Sandella, you haven't been boring God.

—JEAN HOUSTON, PHD, author, speaker, philosopher

Goodbye, Hurt and Pain is a necessary handbook for anyone who would like to hit the reset button on your life. Sandella interweaves the best of neuroscience, psychology, and her own experience in a fascinating book of emotional discovery. Thanks to this brilliant book, your regenerated self can rise above the ashes of the past into a world of hope and new possibilities.

—CONSTANCE BUFFALO, president, Renaissance Project, Intl.

Goodbye,
Hurt & Pain

Goodbye,
Hurt & Pain

*7 Simple Steps for
Health, Love, and Success*

DEBORAH SANDELLA, PHD, RN

Conari Press

This edition first published in 2016 by Conari Press, an imprint of
Red Wheel/Weiser, LLC

With offices at:
65 Parker Street, Suite 7
Newburyport, MA 01950
www.redwheelweiser.com

ISBN: 978-1-57324-678-1

Library of Congress Cataloging-in-Publication Data
Names: Sandella, Deborah L., author.
Title: Goodbye, hurt and pain: 7 simple steps for health, love, and success
 / Deborah Sandella, PhD, RN.
Description: Newburyport, MA : Conari Press, an imprint of Red Wheel/Weiser,
 LLC, [2016] | Includes bibliographical references and index.
Identifiers: LCCN 2016006299 | ISBN 9781573246781 (5.5 x 8.5 tp : alk. paper)
Subjects: LCSH: Imagery (Psychology)--Therapeutic use. |
 Visualization—Therapeutic use. | Mind and body. | Memory. | Emotions.
Classification: LCC RC489.F35 S27 2016 | DDC 615.8/51—dc23
LC record available at https://lccn.loc.gov/2016006299

Cover design by Mark Gelotte, www.markgelotte.com
Cover photograph © art4all/shutterstock
Interior illustrations by Mark Gelotte
Interior by Maureen Forys, Happenstance Type-O-Rama
Typeset in Warnock Pro and Karmina Sans

Printed in the United States of America
MG

10 9 8 7 6 5 4 3 2 1

This book is dedicated to the courageous and loving women upon whose shoulders I stand:

My mother, Imogene Scroggins Sandella, who married at age nineteen, finished college at fifty, and as a creative administrator into her sixties, saved our small-town hospital when most were failing. She taught me you're never too young or too old to make a difference. At eighty-seven, she continues to be a loving presence.

PHOTO BY LINDSEY SANDELLA-GREER

My paternal grandmother "Nona," Filomena Torchia Sandella, who traveled solo from Paterno, Italy, to the United States at sixteen, married and birthed eleven children, raising the surviving seven in a house absent indoor plumbing. Unable to read or write, she inspires me as a living example of the commonsense wisdom in each of us, regardless of education and wealth.

CONTENTS

FOREWORD

Having spent time working as a schoolteacher, teacher trainer, psychotherapist, success coach, and human potential trainer, I have witnessed the immense influence that feelings have on a person's performance and mood. From the first time Deborah Sandella ("Dr. Deb" as her students call her) introduced me to her RIM work (RIM stands for "Regenerating Images in Memory"), I saw its powerful potential to create immediate and dramatic physical and behavioral changes in people. And I have continued to witness this time after time, year after year, as she and her facilitators work with my students.

Having known and worked with Deb for over eleven years, first as my student and later as my friend and coauthor, I'm delighted to introduce her new book to you. Every once in a while, you read a book that has a profound personal impact on you. This book will do that. It is written from the heart in a down-to-earth way that will touch you intimately—and probably change your life.

Deb's passion and pioneering spirit have led to her discoveries of how to help people more easily uncover that place within us that knows the answers to every one of our deepest questions. Her commitment to continually expand her understanding of the natural self-healing mechanisms operating in us has resulted in this wonderful and profound book.

Goodbye, Hurt and Pain will introduce you to seven powerful discoveries of how to master your feelings, and when you consistently apply them, you can expect to live a dynamic life of ever-expanding success and happiness.

In fact, because this work produces such immediate and extraordinary emotional and physical results, it may at first appear unbelievable, but I have witnessed it in action in my own life and the lives of hundreds of my students and trainees and can testify to its profound impact.

I've come to respect Dr. Deb's quiet power as she courageously walks clients through the darkness of their most devastating and painful memories and into the light of new confidence, emotional freedom, and personal power. She consistently affirms and awakens in them their innate resourcefulness. In person you can see and feel it in her energetic presence and gaze. Now you have the opportunity to feel it through her writing.

As you read this book, I encourage you to dive headfirst into the Practice It Yourself activities. I promise you that the rewards will be well worth it. You will move beyond what you've previously thought possible. All you have to do is follow the step-by-step process that Dr. Deb leads you through, and you'll see your life growing more successful and fulfilling every day.

To Your Success,
Jack Canfield

CEO of the Canfield Training Group; cocreator of the Chicken Soup for the Soul® Series; coauthor of The Success Principles™; internationally renowned corporate trainer, keynote speaker, and popular radio and TV talk show guest

INTRODUCTION

The phone rings, and I sleepily pick up the receiver. It feels like a dream as I hear my brother's heavy words: "Dad's suffered a cardiac arrest and he's in the ICU." He has received every possible drug, but his blood pressure isn't holding. The nurses feel sure he can't survive the night, so they have requested a "do not resuscitate" agreement.

In my mind, I hear myself reacting to the nurses: "*How can you even ask that question? You have no idea who this man is, how special he is to his whole community.*" In this moment, something snaps, and I say, "No, I won't agree." Having started my career as a nurse, my response is completely out of character, but an intuitive process is taking over.

As I walk back to bed, I am visited by a spontaneous vision. I see my dad with his back to me as he walks off toward the horizon. I am there angrily yelling: "*I'm so mad at you for leaving. I'm not ready for you to go. I have so many more things I want us to share.*" To my complete surprise, he pauses and turns to face me. His countenance is radiant with a gentle expression I have never seen before when he says in a kind voice: "*I didn't know you felt that way; okay.*"

As my body senses his words, the anger instantly drains away, and I feel like a wet noodle. At the same time, my logical mind remarks with a statement and question: "*All this is just in my head, right?*" As I climb back into bed, I feel an urging to keep his image in my awareness, like an earthly lifeline to his spirit.

The next day I fly to rural Kansas and walk into ICU. The nursing staff report: "Sometime in the middle of the night, your dad's blood pressure began to hold." Encouraged, I sit at his bedside over several nights. I am compelled to imagine the inside of his unconscious body. His lungs appear foggy gray with darker, heavy guck at the bottom. Feeling I would do anything to help him survive, I shed my professional academic image and begin to experiment. Initially, I imagine him breathing in clean, fresh air and exhaling gray darkness. This seems to lighten it a bit, but I can tell it is fatiguing him so I stop.

Next I begin breathing for him. I imagine fresh air filling his lungs, displacing the heavy grayness, which is displaced with each exhale. I become the "breather" as he lies relaxed and unconscious in his hospital bed. Gradually, in my mind's eye I see his lungs fill with bright, blue sky and the grayness is gone except for a solid black spot at the base of his lungs. No matter how hard I try, it remains.

The next morning, the pulmonologist visits and says Dad's lungs actually look good, except for a bit of aspirated solid material at the base. Fortunately, the doctor can mechanically remove the material with a bronchoscope. Although Dad's oxygen levels return to normal after the procedure, the doctor cautions us against false optimism: "I wouldn't get your hopes up. Your dad's brain was without oxygen for a long time, and he's probably suffered brain damage." Ignoring his caution, I feel encouraged that my intuitive sensing has been accurate, and I begin imagining Dad's vital brain.

The epilogue to my dad's story is that he did survive and, to the complete surprise of the hospital staff, returned with normal mental capacity. He lived five more vibrant years—a time he and my mom said was the best of their lives. We had a second chance and we took it. The results were extraordinary.[1]

As a doctoral-level health care professional who had done research and taught at the University of Colorado, I could not make sense of this experience. It just didn't compute; it defied everything I had learned about medicine. Yet these imagined experiences were more important to me than all of my numerous years of education, and I committed to understanding how to harness this remarkable power for intentional emotional and physical healing.

Twenty years later, I've learned that imagination is an extraordinary resource within each of us with powers not found in our ordinary thought processes. It is our birthright and so simple that we tend to dismiss it too easily—as if it were child's play. Yet, the extraordinary emotional and physical results I have witnessed speak for themselves. The RIM Method and this book are the culmination of this journey.

DYNAMICS BETWEEN FEELINGS, THE BODY, AND IMAGINATION

Since the dawn of human time, we have been scared of undesirable feelings. The story of Adam and Eve demonstrates how acting on one's feelings leads to dangerous outcomes. Socrates and Aristotle wrote revered philosophy on how we should cultivate an independent personality, never lowering ourselves to the emotions of anger and lust. Somewhere along the way, we came to think that our feelings were in need of policing to assure our acceptance as virtuous people.

We don't like negative feelings because they are emotionally and physically uncomfortable. This instinct isn't wrong. Recent research shows negative feelings that become chronic can impact our health. Susan Everson-Rose, an associate professor of medicine at the University of Minnesota, along with her associates, found that depression raised the risk of stroke or ministroke by 86 percent, chronic stress increased it 59 percent, while hostility doubled the risk. These findings for the 7,000 adults ages 45–84 in the study remained constant over eight and a half years even when age, race, sex, health behaviors, and other known risk factors were taken into account. At the start, none of the subjects had experienced a stroke or ministroke. The authors conclude that if we want to prevent strokes, we need to pay attention to stress and emotions and how they affect us.[2]

Similarly, Emory University researchers reviewed 3,200 coronary angiography patients and found that women under fifty-five with depression had twice the risk of dying from a heart condition or experiencing a heart attack.[3]

The American Institute of Stress, which reviews stress research, estimates that stress-related and stress-induced illnesses account for 75–90% of the one-billion visits Americans make to the doctor annually.[4] And Madhu Kalia from Thomas Jefferson University suggests that disabilities caused by stress are just as great as the disabilities caused by workplace accidents or other common medical conditions such as hypertension, diabetes, and arthritis.[5]

What are we to do? Feelings have a spontaneous life of their own, and if painful ones become chronic, they cause emotional and physical suffering and harm.

In 1995, Daniel Goleman's groundbreaking book *Emotional Intelligence, Why It Can Matter More than IQ* established the radical importance of emotions. He showed how *feeling* frequently trumps *thinking* as an automatic response to life. This bias develops because the emotional brain existed long before the rational brain, "which gives evolved emotional centers immense power to influence the functioning of the rest of the brain—including its centers for thought."[6] Furthermore, the emotional part of the brain learns in a different way from the logical part.

Success or failure in your work and relationships is dependent on how you manage your feelings. The trouble is, precious few of us stop to think about what we're feeling. Our attention is drawn instead to activity around us while our unnoticed inner state initiates most of our behavior. In other words, our reflexive reactions are largely motivated by feelings to which we pay little attention. This is not a recipe for success.

If I were to ask you, "What are you feeling right now?" would you know? Unless you're in the middle of an emotional event, chances are your answer would be, "I have no idea." Roget's Thesaurus includes more than 3,000 words related to emotion, yet most of us are intimidated by our personal psychology because it's invisible and uncontrollable. So, we avoid thinking about how we feel, while at the same time, we can't stop thinking about how we feel. That's quite an interesting paradox.

So how do we begin to bring our feelings into our conscious awareness? And then how do we allow them to evaporate? You're holding the answer in your hands.

MIND TO MATTER

Do you ever feel overwhelmed by uncomfortable emotions? As if they have consumed you? Everyone has experienced this at one time or another. Because feelings are perceived as unseen and uncontrollable, they can seem like scary ghosts chasing us no matter how much we want them gone. Yet when we give form to our feelings, they suddenly have boundaries. When emotions are measurable, the mind accepts them rather than ignoring them.

What is the color of love? How heavy is sadness? What is the size of anger or the density of pain? *Goodbye, Hurt and Pain* will help you imagine the form and function of your feelings by looking through an organic lens. Mother Nature is a great teacher with the awe-inspiring workings of the Universe. We, too, are created with life's inherent sense of order and urge to thrive. Since our bodies are a reflection of Nature, we can use the natural world as a metaphor to solve our problems. As early as 1452, men studied birds closely in order to understand flight;

the Wright brothers gained insight from observing pigeons when designing the first airplane.[7] This concept is now a scientific discipline called *biomimicry*, which comes from the Greek words *bios* for "life" and *mimesis* "to imitate." Similarly, *Goodbye, Hurt and Pain* uses Nature as metaphor to comprehend emotions better.

Physics is one of the oldest explored natural sciences—the study of matter and its motion through space and time, along with related concepts of energy and force. In general, physics helps us understand how the universe behaves. *Goodbye, Hurt and Pain* uses processes in physics as metaphors to give shape and movement to invisible emotions, similar to the way scientists imagined invisible forces like gravity, electricity, and electromagnetism even before their existence was proven. As feelings take form, the rational brain engages with matters of the heart, and our emotions become manageable in ways we've not considered until now.

Emotions predictably expand and contract, and throughout this book we'll look at how taming big, uncomfortable, invisible feelings and memories can help you gain an exhilarating sense of emotional mastery. Once you know how to dial in to your feelings, your native emotional intelligence begins to respond much like a self-cleaning oven, problem-solver, and success magnet. And results come quickly. You will find yourself resolving deep-rooted problems and manifesting your dreams at speeds as fast as Google search results. Again, the answers originate outside the logical mind.

You'll learn how emotions work—and how to have yours working effortlessly for you—through recent neuroscientific findings and compelling real-life stories. You will also have an opportunity to practice ramping up your own emotional intelligence through Practice It Yourself sections at the end of each chapter.

HOW I CAME TO THESE METHODS: THE STORY OF RIM

It's 1998, the phone rings, and it's my client Ellie, checking in to see if I've reopened my psychotherapy practice as planned. It's no surprise that she's calling because her work is unfinished; she's the only client I had referred to another therapist before I left on a family sabbatical to Australia. We talk, and as I hang up, I hear a voice say: "*If you go back to doing what you used to do, you'll get sick.*" I stop in my tracks and wonder: "*Who said that?*" It definitely wasn't my client, and it certainly wasn't my conscious mind. If this is my intuition speaking, it's a total surprise! Ah, I remember that's how true intuition works—it drops in without preceding thought or emotion.

This turning point in my career took me places I never expected. Like Dorothy in the *Wizard of Oz*, I was setting out on an adventure, moving toward something new and exciting, something I didn't know and to which I was strongly drawn. It turns out I was on a quest to discover an inventive way of working with feelings. And discover it I did.

When I began exploring a new way of processing emotions, I set aside expectations of what I believed *possible* and *impossible*. Rather, I decided to let clients show their capacities without limits. I have been amazed at the results. In fact, the speed of remarkable change in the real-life stories shared in these pages can seem almost too rapid to be believed. I and others have witnessed it time and time again. Their stories lend credence to the immense inner resilience in all of us. This evidence convincingly shows that we have a reliable system capable of processing life's experiences of pain and doubt more quickly and effectively than we previously thought. Our natural curiosity and joy can be felt more easily than we have ever considered. We just need to understand the inner code.

For the past twenty years I have been using the techniques you'll find in this book and training facilitators around the world to use them as well. We have all been continually astonished at how well they work—and how quickly. RIM student Steve Torneten received this note from a local real estate agent who had volunteered for a practice session: "I'm not sure what you did, but I've had six properties go under contract since then—about $995K of commissions. Thank you, thank you, thank you!" Similarly, another student Stephanie did a practice session with her fitness trainer. He was so grateful for his results, he gave her twelve free sessions.

The RIM in the RIM Method stands for Regenerating Images in Memory (RIM®), and the real-life stories of client experiences in this book have been guided by myself or certified facilitators I have trained. Although every story is authentic, client identities are protected, and their narratives have been condensed to only the critical moments in their RIM experiences.

RIM introduces a new paradigm or novel view of how our emotional system works. Turning away from the idea that painful experiences and feelings fracture or permanently damage you, RIM works on the principle that you have an emotional operating system that organically knows how to deepen positive feelings and dissolve painful ones. Given this inherent internal resourcefulness, the process is client-generated and guided by inner sensation and imagination. The many stories you read in this book will grow your conscious and unconscious expectation of what's possible. As your belief expands, greater personal results become possible. You may decide to go on this adventure with a book club. Transformation is easier and more fun when shared.

Since RIM is nonlinear (not protocol or logic driven), your left brain may be frustrated because it's used to knowing what to expect. Although that's how the rational mind works, it's not the nature of the unconscious, which has a mind of its own.

To learn more about how RIM works, take a look at the Questions & Answers section at the back of the book. But there's more: your purchase of this book includes a gift of an audio meditation of a Practice It Yourself session, so you can bring the process alive in the comfort of your own home. Find this gift and others at *www.GoodbyeHurtandPain.com*.

Congratulations, you are on a personal quest to clear hidden, stuck emotion that has been stopping you from having what you want. By reading this book, you are freeing yourself to have your best life. In the coming pages, you'll learn seven exhilarating discoveries about your emotions; this self-understanding will change the way you see yourself and the power of your inner resources. The amazing real-life stories will expand your conscious thinking and unconscious beliefs to allow you to trust that saying goodbye to painful feelings and memories is easier than you've ever imagined. You'll learn to

- trust the organic expiration of frightening feelings
- quickly reduce overwhelming emotion to controllable form
- unstick uncomfortable feelings
- neutralize the magnetic charge of repetitive harmful behavior
- find the gift of beauty in ugly feelings
- uncover and express the sensation of wholeness through your mind and body

- reconstitute memory for greater safety and aliveness
- renew your emotional equilibrium whenever you need to
- master emotions in the blink of an eye

Some of you will use this book to generate empowering changes within yourself. Some will change your lives in ways you didn't think possible. If you wish to be such a reader, set aside your expectations of what's possible. Enter these lessons with an open mind and welcome what you read as personally attainable. If you find yourself doubting or confused, persevere by engaging in the Practice It Yourself sessions regularly and often.

Though I write with intention, your subjective reading has a life of its own—it's yours to experience. . . . Enjoy!

FLOW & GO

Your Feelings Have a Natural Shelf Life

> *Life is like riding a bicycle. To keep your balance, you must keep moving.* —ALBERT EINSTEIN

> *Your intellect may be confused, but your emotions will never lie to you.* —ROGER EBERT

> *The deeper that sorrow carves into your being, the more joy you can contain.* —KHALIL GIBRAN

When you allow the organic flow of feelings, they bring valuable information and naturally expire as you move effortlessly forward. Kris, John, and Nancy show you how it works in the following stories.

KRIS'S STORY: WHEN EMOTIONS GO UNDERGROUND

Kris is a vital forty-nine-year-old manager. Married with two young adult children, she and her husband Rich are filling their empty nest with lots of playfulness. For her birthday, he buys her a beautiful, pink mountain bike, and they head to Moab for an exciting adventure. The sun is shining; the trail is wide open. And then it happens: Kris hits a bump and goes flying. Fortunately, her head is protected by her helmet, but her left leg is shattered on impact. Seeing her tibia poking through the ruptured skin causes her and Rich to grow faint, until Rich comes to his senses and calls for emergency help. Thank God there is cell service.

At the small hospital nearby, Kris lies on a gurney swimming in anxiety when the doctor appears: "Don't worry, Kris, we'll get you stabilized and then send you to Salt Lake for surgery where they have better resources to repair the complexity of this break."

Hearing these words, Kris's anxiety ramps up, and her mind races with unanswerable worries: *"Will I be okay? Will I walk again? Will I have a limp? What's going to happen? If only I had seen that rock on the trail. I can't believe it. Is this really me lying in the ER? Could I be dreaming?"*

As the intensity of her concerns increase, so do her symptoms. Her blood pressure drops, and her chest constricts and tightens. She begins to quiver, and her breathing stops. Panicked like a swimmer inhaling water rather than oxygen, she feels she is dying. *"Help me, help me, somebody help me!"* she screams silently, feeling like she is in one of those dreams where you try to yell and can't!

The ER staff recognizes this is not a panic attack, but something more serious, and quickly treats her for life-threatening anaphylactic shock. As her symptoms recede, she learns she has experienced an allergic reaction to one of the medications.

The next day, Kris is taken by ambulance to a medical center in Salt Lake City. Her surgery is successful, and after a few weeks of rehab, she is discharged home. It soon looks like she is healed and back on track—until she returns to her job and quickly slips into severe depression. For no apparent reason, she is unable to work and her previous enjoyment of life is gone. She goes on anti-depressants, yet the depression does not lift.

When her husband Rich contacts me for an appointment for Kris, he sounds desperate. It has been months since she's been off work and nothing is helping; in fact, nothing is changing the least bit.

As Kris sits with closed eyes, she senses a weird feeling in her stomach. Focusing attention on it, she describes it as a black swirling inside that is trying to suck her in and she is afraid of disappearing.

I ask Kris's imagination to call in an image of someone to be a comforting and safe traveler with her on this journey, and her mother shows up. With Mom, she feels safe to bravely move into the black vortex and ride it around and down to the source. As they swirl downward, Kris begins to feel intense dizziness and nausea. Surrendering to the feeling, she and Mom glide down until they hit bottom in an image of the first ER room where she almost died. Watching herself in the scene, she sees Kris lying on the gurney with a broken leg and eyes frozen wide in terror.

Gazing into her own eyes, she begins to cry, even sob:

I thought I was dying . . . I thought I'd never see my kids again . . . Never again to enjoy the beauty of the mountains and sunshine. I thought it was over—I thought my life was over. If I tried hard enough maybe I could hold on—but I couldn't—my chest was getting tighter and tighter and I couldn't breathe. No matter how hard I tried, I couldn't force in another breath. I was dying.

Moving her attention into this image and bringing her mother with her, Kris hesitantly looks out of these terrified eyes and senses the feeling of dying. She moves into this emotional experience as if it were today, and her awareness sits in it, as it organically recedes after a few minutes. Soon there's room for remembering the reality of her physical recovery. Slowly and naturally the frozen feeling of dying melts, and her appreciation for life returns. The feeling of being stuck in a horrible memory has been brought forward, allowed, and organically released. Life has come back!

After this deeply visceral expression of terror, Kris's symptoms of severe depression disappear, and she gradually returns to her job and her life. She finally feels the gratitude for surviving the biking accident she couldn't authentically experience while she was emotionally stuck between life and death. The previously stuck memory has been integrated, and she is present again.

Kris's story demonstrates how unprocessed intense emotion goes underground and creates a subconscious block even when the original traumatic event resolves. Furthermore, her journey shows how health can be regained as soon as the original event is integrated in the mind, heart, and body.

JOHN'S STORY: WELCOMING THE HIDDEN MESSAGES IN PAIN

Rheumatoid arthritis struck John when he was in his early forties. Now fifty, his hands are misshapen, his sleeping severely interrupted, and he takes pain relievers daily as frequently as permitted. Feeling oppressed by his physical condition, John requests help. As he closes his eyes to sense his body, the first thing to attract his attention is discomfort around his neck and left ear. Instead of following his usual habit to medicate, he focuses on the pain, and there comes a subtle lessening of the physical pressure. As he moves his awareness into this painful area, the discomfort gradually dissolves, and he feels a sense of calm.

As he practices moving into the pain and listening during several monthly sessions, John notices that spontaneous insights sometimes pop up: "I need to slow down. I'm doing too much," or "I'm angry with my wife. She hurt my feelings when she said I wasn't trying to lose weight. How can I talk with her about it and say it so she'll hear me instead of getting defensive?"

When he is not constantly trying to get rid of the pain, John begins to respect it as a message from his body. As he starts to value his true feelings, he notices a corresponding change in his medication use: he doesn't need it the same way. In fact he goes from using analgesics 24/7 to one to two times a week, primarily when he's excessively tired.

Over time, these insights cause John to change other habits as well. He begins to eat healthier foods and to communicate more honestly when there is a conflict with family members or employees. He speaks up instead of avoiding issues and thus begins to feel a sense of personal power for the first time in his life.

As John continues a collaborative relationship with the pain, he grows happier, healthier, thinner, and better able to navigate relationships. He quits trying to stop the pain and sees it as an expression of his hidden, authentic feelings. John has freed himself from the oppression of illness. Instead, he receives the symptoms as helpful feedback guiding him to live a healthier and happier life. His story demonstrates how welcoming emotions hidden in physical pain brings helpful insights and lessens physical discomfort. Our bodies naturally give a voice to those things within that need our attention. We merely have to listen and heed the messages.

NANCY'S STORY: HOW OUR FEELINGS HELP KEEP US SAFE

We've all known people who genuinely sense and authentically share their emotions without hesitation, freely expressing what they feel. Nancy is one of these people. What you see is what you get. She doesn't beat around the bush. Having known Nancy over many years, I can tell you that the outcome of her way of being is evident.

For example, when she was a young psychotherapist at a community mental health center, she volunteered for a research project that paired difficult teens with therapists to climb and rappel nearby mountains weekly for six weeks. The project was going very well, and Nancy enjoyed this unique way of interacting with her young clients. She also discovered she loved rappelling! No wallflower here, Nancy enjoyed thrill-seeking.

On one of the group's outings, she stood on the top of a cliff looking down into a narrow canyon between two steep mountains. When it was her turn to descend, she just couldn't do it, even though she had done so gleefully in the past. In her honest and natural style, she expressed her fear to the climbing guides—her body was refusing to go. They decided to check her equipment and found a disconnected rope—the rope that would have suspended her body, in fact. If she had gone over the edge, she might have fallen to her death.

Nancy is a beautiful example of how the intelligence of our organic, body-centered emotion knows more than our intellectual mind. When we pay attention and listen instead of denying, suppressing, fearing, or disliking our spontaneous feelings, we gain great access to our natural intuition (knowing something without understanding how we know it). Nancy's experience demonstrates how our inherent feelings help keep us safe in spite of what the logical mind thinks. It's wonderful to know the power we possess!

HOW IT WORKS—PRACTICALLY AND SCIENTIFICALLY

We frequently speak of our feelings as if we *are* them. You hear it in our patterns of speech: "I am angry," as if to say, "I am anger." However, feelings naturally arise as passing states of awareness and are not part of us. Rather, they give feedback and then expire. Think of it as similar to how a thermometer measures our internal body temperature at 9:00 a.m. at a healthy 98.6 and, three hours later when we are getting the flu, it registers 101.5. The feedback that we have a fever allows us to make an informed decision about whether to take fever-reducing meds, call the doctor, or go to bed and wait it out. A feverish reading is temporary and will change. In the same way, our emotional temperature fluctuates depending on external and internal events and our reaction to them. Looking back at Kris's real-life story, we see how her bike accident and life-threatening allergic reaction created intense emotions that would have been temporary if she had not gotten stuck.

The origin of the word *emotion* is the 1570–80 Middle French word *esmotion* from *movoir* or motion; thus, *esmovoir* means "to set in motion or move the feelings."[1] The essential function of feelings is to provide feedback and pass through us organically like water flows in a river. In the same way water moves through the atmosphere, in and out of oceans, over and under land, human feelings continuously precipitate, go underground, rise to the surface, and evaporate through our awareness.

Trying to control our feelings through resistance and avoidance is like damming a river to stop the flow. An emotional dam pools feelings. This reservoir of avoided emotion remains in the body until we release it. In other words, the feelings we tried to avoid get held inside us instead. We hold on to what we are trying to avoid. Life constantly challenges us; it's not personal, just the natural process of growth and evolution. The stories of John and Kris demonstrate how easy it is to build emotional dams. Many times the process happens without us realizing it—until a symptom or illness gets our attention.

What emotional dams do you have in place? Distrust after a divorce? Shutting down emotionally after a job loss? Doubting yourself after a personal or professional rejection? Obsessing about safety after an accident? Let's explore the source of some emotional dams to gain more insight into how they operate in our lives.

Emotions Flow Naturally

A range of feeling from the highest high to the lowest low is a normal aspect of our organic emotional system. Each passing feeling arises spontaneously, brings valuable information, and then evaporates. When we allow and recognize this flow, we activate self-recovery. Since everyone's emotional state directly influences success in relationships, work, and health, we gain an ability to produce desired outcomes by allowing our feelings to expire naturally without damming or flooding. Looking through a metaphoric lens, we are the riverbank, and the water flowing through us is emotion. We are stable and solid, while the feelings moving through us are constantly changing. We are emotionally dynamic beings. Sometimes emotion is gentle, like rain feeding the river to nourish life; sometimes it explodes like a rainstorm whose floodwaters wipe out bridges and homes.

You don't have to try to feel your emotions; they have their own momentum. Think of the lyrics in Jennifer Love Hewitt's *Don't Push the River*. On the other hand, when you build dams, the natural emotional flow toward expiration is blocked. Remember you can always choose to stop building dams so that your emotional flow expires as it was meant to.

Whether you dam up your feelings or allow them to run freely is your choice. But make no mistake: how you manage the flow has consequences. When you learn to recognize and understand the nature of your undesirable feelings, you can allow their safe expiration and devise floodgates to discharge intense ones in safe ways that prevent emotional flooding.

Our Three Primal Feelings: Curiosity, Comfort, and Discomfort

We are born with three primal emotional states: curiosity, comfort, and discomfort. You can easily observe them in infants even though they cannot understand or verbalize their internal experience or thoughts. We come programmed with these neurological receptors.

Take curiosity, for example. Researcher Hildy Ross at the University of Waterloo, Ontario, found that a group of twelve-month-olds consistently preferred new toys to familiar ones and spent more time manipulating the complex array of toys rather than the simple ones.[2] These findings suggest that we come into the world as explorers. That makes sense when we see how determined babies are to do whatever it takes to walk. If you have spent any time observing infants and toddlers, their curiosity is obvious—hence the large array of baby-proofing gadgets available to us.

Similarly, you do not have to be a researcher to know when an alert baby is comfortable. They have the curious glint in the eyes, the smile that tugs at your heart, and the sounds of squealing, gurgling, and laughing that create sympathetic delight in your body. You can sense an infant's spontaneous happiness without words. In fact, the joyful sight and sounds of a happy baby are contagious. Pay attention when you hear a baby cooing or a child laughing, and notice how your body responds. I remember once sitting on an airplane when a toddler's uncontainable giggles became audible in the silence immediately after landing. All of us began to make knowing eye contact and smiling at one another. As the spontaneous sounds continued to fill the cabin, our adult smiles finally burst into audible laughter. We just couldn't help ourselves. We all walked off the plane feeling great!

Although infants cannot tell us about their discomfort in words like older children, they give clues through their bodies. Pain is communicated through babies' bodies in changes to heart rate, breathing rate, and blood pressure. Infants act differently when they are in pain than when they are comfortable. Although each infant responds individually and may be inconsistent, there are certain behaviors like fussing, crying, furrowed brow, squeezed-shut eyes, and a quivering chin that reflect discomfort.

Discomfort is a visceral or physiological experience even when the source is emotional. Neuroanatomist A. D. Craig suggests the definition of human emotion to be both a subjective feeling and a body experience. He points out that, given this insight, emotions are not simply occasional events, but ongoing and continuous, even when they go unnoticed as unconscious human emotional acts.[3] In other words, our feelings are constantly changing and creating different body experiences even when we are oblivious to them.

Although you may not remember your very early experiences, you too were born with the three spontaneous states of curiosity, comfort, and discomfort. Through the years you have evolved more complex feelings, but these primal emotions still strongly motivate behavior. As a growing baby, then child, you organically sought intuitive ways to maintain comfort. It all happened through your body, not your head, because your intellectual mind was immature.

The techniques you learn in this book will show you how to unravel primal discomfort dammed in your body. As it quickly and naturally evaporates, you can remember your inherent curiosity and childlike joy, regardless of age.

The Most Commonly Dammed or "Damned" Feelings

As adults, our central motivators continue to be maintaining comfort and avoiding discomfort. It is no surprise, then, that emotions that get dammed up consciously and unconsciously are related to discomfort. They are those we consider "negative," such as fear, anger, sadness/grief, and envy. These are the emotions we often avoid, forget, resist, ignore, bury, and control because they are uncomfortable. Those young and old alike who have not learned to delay gratification demonstrate how strongly we want what we want and don't want what we don't want. Just observe the persistent drive in young children to get their way.

Fear

One primal discomfort is fear. When we feel afraid, there is a disturbance in our body, mind, and spirit. The fear stimulated by chest pain and shortness of breath in panic attacks highlights the direct connection between our bodies and emotions that bypasses thinking. Feelings acting through our bodies can be quite convincing in making us feel we are dying.

Fear expresses in various ways depending on personality and beliefs about the world. An acutely fearful experience elicits a biochemical reaction that expresses as fight, flight, freeze, or faint. When your concern is about future safety, anxiety arises. Fear directed to past experiences results in shame, regret, and guilt.

What is your initial response to fear? Your secondary response? As you look back over your life, you will notice whether you have a tendency to flee, fight, freeze, or faint. None of these responses is better or worse; each is a natural pattern of responding given your genetic predisposition and life experiences. By identifying reflective habits, you can compassionately understand yourself and realize you have additional choices to feel comfortable.

Anger

Within anger is an implicit fear of loss of control/comfort—like a child throwing a temper tantrum: "Something's not going my way, and I don't like it." Yes, our infantile need for comfort continues regardless of age. The good news is when the crying baby in us gets loud, our adult self can listen, soothe, and learn to understand the cause.

Anger is commonly misunderstood. Synonyms that surface in an online thesaurus search describe *anger* as a very strong attitude: "bitterness, cantankerousness, vexation, acrimony, antagonism, violence, peevishness, petulance, ill humor, ill temper."

Do you sense the implication? There is a subtle suggestion the angry person has a difficult personality. Who wants to be labeled that way? Over the years, many of us have learned to shut off feelings of anger for fear of sounding ill-tempered, demanding, and antagonistic.

Growing up with a first-generation Italian father, my childhood experiences with raw anger were somewhat frightening. When I visited Italy in college, I witnessed angry outbursts frequently and began to understand my dad. The dramatic verbal expression of anger I saw there is common and fleeting; it is not necessarily personal or threatening. In fact, you frequently see it between people who are strangers on Italian streets. It is a dramatic acknowledgment that something has happened you did not expect and do not like. The speaker lets it be known in a passionate voice that there is a perceived offense, and then it is done. It is interesting to note that in stroke research anger did not increase the risk of stroke or ministroke, but *hostility* did. Anger like I saw in Italy is fleeting, whereas hostility is enduring. Furthermore, the incidence of stroke in southern Italy where my grandparents grew up is significantly lower than in other European countries.[4] (Diet differences, however, were not considered in the study.)

Anger, like all emotion, is feedback from our built-in navigational system. It warns us we may be facing a potential violation externally or internally. As we understand from hardwired home security systems, most violations are false alarms without an actual intruder, but we just don't know until we investigate. Though rare, when a real burglar is in the area, we definitely want to be alerted so we can protect ourselves. Anger operates like a personal emotional security system. Feelings of anger warn you something dangerous could happen and further investigation is indicated to determine if action is needed to stay safe.

You can see how disregarding angry feelings may keep you from recognizing a real violation in your midst and you could get hurt. In fact, Siegman and Smith, editors of *Anger, Hostility, and the Heart,* found when they reviewed the literature preceding 2013 that *repressed* anger is associated with autoimmune diseases.[5]

I remember that in my early twenties as a single, "nice Catholic girl" afraid of being "bitchy," I distanced myself from any hint of rising anger. As a result, I constantly felt confused. Clarity about friends and dating relationships evaded me, and I frequently postponed discerning decisions because I was living in a blur. Eventually, the influence of the women's movement dissolved these old assumptions, and I grew brave enough to sense and acknowledge angry feelings. Wow! What a breakthrough. I finally knew enough about myself to trust I could keep myself safe—my feelings would tell me when I needed to investigate. I was empowered to determine who/what was safe or not.

On the other hand, assuming all anger means a real burglar is in your midst is inaccurate and will lead you to feel the world is a more dangerous place than it is, which could compromise a healthy sense of trust. When we constantly assess our anger as a real violation without investigation, it snowballs into an *attitude* of anger or *hostility,* defined by researchers Siegman and Smith as a cynical and negative expectation of life. Their review of previous studies finds hostility to be associated with coronary heart disease (CHD).

An interesting 2015 study analyzed language used on Twitter and found that people reflecting "negative emotions—especially anger—were at significantly greater risk for cardiovascular mortality" than those with positive emotional language patterns. The study controlled for income and education factors. The researchers suggest: "A cross-sectional regression model based only on Twitter language predicted AHD [atherosclerotic heart disease] mortality significantly better than did a model that combined ten common demographic, socioeconomic, and health risk factors including smoking, diabetes, hypertension, and obesity."[6]

Siegman and Smith further found that verbally sharing anger is positive and insightful, while an explosive, aggressive expression of anger is toxic to the heart. The research identifies the dangerous element to be aggressiveness, while Raymond A. DiGiuseppe, coauthor of the 2006 book *Understanding Anger Disorders,* finds revenge is the major driver of whether someone will behave in an aggressive way. He says it's hard to change such people with anger management classes because they feel justified in their feeling.[7]

Interestingly, the research reflects a significant difference between how men and women handle similar levels of anger, with men scoring higher on "aggressive expression of anger." Men show higher levels of "hostility" in comparison to women who are more likely to express their anger in a "communicative fashion." The male editors share a powerful conclusion: "It is not at all unreasonable to suggest that gender differences in anger-hostility may account for the gender differences in coronary heart disease."[8]

Anger is feedback from the psyche and body that suggests you pay attention and investigate further to see what's happening because, although an uncommon occurrence, your safety could be jeopardized. When anger is fully allowed and understood, it becomes mobilizing, and decisions can be made that assure emotional and physical health. Twenty years of witnessing clients dealing with anger through the RIM process has shown me that identifying the underlying source of anger rapidly accelerates an understanding of what's happening and whether there is real danger and what action, if any, is indicated.

For example, Mary was referred to me by her acupuncturist because she continued to experience physical symptoms secondary to intense, ongoing anger with her ex-husband, though they had been divorced for six years. He had remarried, but she still was so caught up in hating him for cheating on her, she was unable to enjoy her life. When Mary closed her eyes, followed her attention into her body, and sensed the energy of anger there, she saw it was like a smoldering volcano.

As she acknowledged and greeted this hostile energy she was carrying in her body, the tension began to release. She talked freely to her imagined ex-husband without fear of retaliation or rejection. Gradually, as the emotion poured from her body through her words, she felt some inner openness. She had been holding a tightly wound ball of fury for a long time, and it had taken up a lot of room and required constant energy to contain. With this gut-level emptying of pent-up anger, Mary began to breathe more easily. Her thinking began to relax, and she had spontaneous insights of how she had contributed to the breakup of the marriage. Surprised and able to see she was not just a helpless victim, Mary felt lighter and freer. At the end of her process, she felt ready to begin living her own life in a joyful way.

Her imagination also shared how their young daughter was in need of more fun. Through the unfolding imagery, Mary saw how her hostility was preventing playful interactions. Although regret came with this new awareness, she now felt she could spend time with her daughter differently.

The week after Mary's single session, a follow-up message came from her referral source: "OMG, whatever happened with Mary must have been powerful. Right after her session, she called her ex-husband and apologized to him for her part in the breakup of their relationship, and now she is a different woman!"

Hurt and Anger

Anger and hurt are two sides of the same coin. Depending on your unique personality and life events, you spontaneously feel one of them first, but they are stacked. For example, Mary was stuck in her anger at being betrayed. As she dived into it and gave it a voice, she uncovered the deeper hurt. Previously, she had only allowed herself to experience the anger.

Many women feel hurt first because they are uncomfortable with anger. Dipping into their depths, they eventually discover the anger. Barbara was deeply hurt that her stepdad had sexually abused her as a child. She could not understand why and tended to blame herself. When she found the hurt in her body and allowed it, she was also able to sense the underlying and appropriate indignant anger—*"How could he be so narcissistic?"* and *"Where was Mom?"* With a feeling of safety created through imagination, she could voice her angry feelings directly without risking emotional or physical retaliation. In the experience of standing up for herself for the first time, her countenance transformed from worry and tension to relaxation and beauty. Her appearance, in fact, changed dramatically. The previous hardness that had kept people away vanished, and she felt safe enough to be her true self: smart, soft, and beautiful.

If anger expresses first, it is important to get down to the hurt, and if hurt shows up first, it is important to get down to the anger. Whichever feeling initially surfaces is more comfortable, and the one underneath is less comfortable. Diving into what is less comfortable and surviving unharmed yield resilience and strength.

What is your conditioned take on anger? Did your family welcome such feelings or judge them? Were you punished or made fun of when angry? Did you share your feelings openly or were you ashamed?

What anger is present for you right this minute? Is it indignation at how you've been treated by family, friends, a spouse, an employer, strangers? Take a minute to allow whatever there is to rise to the surface of your mind and take a look at it. Write it down so you can work with it in the Practice It Yourself section at the end of the chapter.

Sadness and Grief

Another set of often dammed feelings is sadness/grief. Who wants to be sad or grieve? No one. Most of us try to avoid these two related feelings at all costs. But sadness and grief are inevitable in this life. Some of us may have more than our share and some less, but it's impossible to live life without them. We all understand loss is a part of living. However, we play games to trick ourselves into believing we can transcend sadness and grief. Though this path may seem to be the high road at the time, it does not take into account the body's reaction—remember, emotional pain is a physical experience. This *visceral* response to discomfort is the nervous system preparing the body to react to stress or an emergency. You may think, "*I'm okay*," but your body is still processing the experience in its own way.

Sadness and grief are sometimes interchangeable, but they usually differ in duration. Sadness can last a few minutes to a few hours and represents a normal response to perceived and actual loss. Grief usually lasts a few weeks to a few years and involves various states of mind over the course of its resolution. Sadness, if extended, may become grief, and grief includes many feelings of sadness.

Putting a name to these feelings makes them sound almost simple: "sadness and grief," so neat and tidy. Of course, nothing could be further from the truth. The internal, subjective experience of loss is indescribably painful—it's the realization that our life can change in a split second and we can lose what we have held close to keep us safe and happy. Grief shatters our illusion of control and involuntarily reveals feelings of helplessness.

Early in my career, a bright, kind thirty-year-old woman I will call Jane taught me a great deal about sadness and grief. Years after her father's death, she was still holding on to the sadness; it was such a strong influence she found herself unable to develop a long-term romantic relationship. As she looked deeply into her connection with her deceased dad, two things became clear. First, she had a wonderfully close rapport with him and he had been her biggest cheerleader. Second, she was clinging to the sadness because it was all that was left of him in a worldly way; it was their last physical connection. She was stuck in a dead feeling about her most loving relationship and unable to move past it because if she did, she thought she would lose what little was left.

As Jane delved deeper, she was able to find the energy of her dad's love permanently imprinted in her heart. By tuning in to her feelings, she could reconnect with his undying affection whenever she chose. Freed from grief, her heart opened. She had her personal cheerleader back. His love again supported her to enjoy life and welcome intimacy with a romantic partner.

Before long, Jane met an attractive young man, fell in love, married, and had a child. It was natural and very tender. She had recovered the feeling of her dad's unconditional love. We both learned that love does not end with physical death.

Elizabeth Kübler-Ross eloquently discerned that grief is a natural process in which we move through five stages: denial, anger, bargaining, depression, and acceptance. When and how we move through each stage is spontaneous and personal. And even though we may wish to avoid all the messiness of it, the body needs to process the experience regardless of what we think. Whether the loss is through death, divorce, rejection, firing, or something personal, the five stages still apply.

The Stages of Grief

DENIAL

The intellectual mind does not seem able to comprehend the instantaneous awareness that something we consider essential is here one minute and gone the next; it defies logic and we resist. Those of us old enough to remember watching television January 28, 1986, all can understand denial from the experience of watching live as the space shuttle *Challenger* launched and broke apart seventy-three seconds into takeoff. The whole country saw the spacecraft disintegrate before our eyes as seven heroic lives evaporated with it. Our brains could not compute. We were shocked, stunned, and immobilized by denial.

ANGER

Next comes the anger: Someone must be at fault—and "How could they!" No matter how mature we are, we go through a stage of wanting to blame someone. After all, if someone is at fault, we might prevent this experience from happening again and save ourselves future suffering. It's a very understandable response, but it doesn't work. No matter how much we want to feel better by being angry, it does not bring back what we have lost.

BARGAINING

Eventually, the mind recovers enough to raise its intellectual voice, and we start negotiating with life, a partner, a boss, a higher power, or just ourselves. Sometimes, we promise to behave better in exchange for a feeling of security instead of grief—"*I'll be a more loving person and never get mad*," "*I'll never drink again*," or "*I'll pray every day*." Other times, we hope to replay the events that occurred in ways that save us from suffering—"*If only I hadn't gone to that party,*" "*If only I had looked into his room when I noticed his door ajar,*" "*If only I had forced him to go to the doctor.*" More than anything, we want some comfort even though we know a different outcome is unattainable.

DEPRESSION

When the mind and body accept that the loss is real and there is no evading it, there is a period of depression—being engulfed in the sadness of life without the lost one. An inevitable sense of reality returns, and it is uncomfortable. It is what it is—significant loss—and there is nothing we can do about it.

ACCEPTANCE

Eventually we come to terms with what is. We reach a place of realizing we can go on, though differently than before—possibilities of a new way of living begin to open up. Joan lost her seventeen-year-old son when a drunk teen in an SUV barreling downhill hit his turning car broadside. When she and I met serendipitously, she shared how her world went black for what felt like forever after her son's tragic death. She continued to feel angry with the driver, who was unhurt in the accident, and

> I knew my life was over and I expected to live forever in a world of blackened death like a completely burnt forest . . . and then out of the blue when I wasn't considering it a possibility, a single blade of grass grew up in the middle of the burnt nothingness. I wanted my son back instead of a new life, but without my permission life took over and I began to live again.

Joan eventually adopted a thirteen-year-old girl from Mexico, and though she did not forget her love for her son, she was reborn. In the same way Nature naturally heals a burned forest, emotional recovery has an organic life of its own. We are designed to thrive.

One of the ways healing works through us is in layers of memory. Even when we have completed the grieving process, deeper levels of sadness and grief may appear years later, triggered by some reminder or similar situation. These are fortuitous times because they bring what was buried and unconscious into view and allow for release. Deeper pain becomes accessible because we have cleared what was there, and now we're ready for another level of lightening the sorrow.

Several months ago, my husband had back surgery. As I sat in the hospital, I became acutely aware of my last experience in a surgery waiting room. It was in 2000, and my dad was having knee-replacement surgery. He suffered a serious stroke the day after surgery and eventually passed away without leaving the hospital. These memories came flooding in as I waited to hear from the doctor. Up came deep feelings of sadness, and I started to cry. Acknowledging and remembering provided a powerful release. As I wrote down my feelings, the sadness gradually dissipated, and I felt clearer and lighter than before.

Receiving the Gift of Old Feelings

Whenever old feelings show up, no matter how old, you have an opportunity to dissolve previously dammed emotion. Instead of thinking you ought to be done with those feelings or that something must be wrong, treat them as dams that you are now strong enough to remove. They offer a door to deeper healing and greater emotional freedom and intelligence.

The RIM processes you will learn about in this book act as a catalyst to bring stuck emotion forward into your conscious awareness so you can set it free to expire naturally, allowing your inherently comfortable self to live again.

As one example, Julie had lost her twenty-five-year-old son Jacob in a skydiving accident fifteen years before she came to see me, and she had been suffering severely ever since. Jacob was her only child, and she and his father had already been divorced for years when Jacob died. Though she was a psychiatric nurse specialist, losing him abruptly created a dam of chronic depression in her. It was like her lifeblood had been sucked out at the time of his death and never returned, that is, until she connected with Jacob through imagination. With eyes closed and his imaginary form before her, she sobbed and shared out loud how she felt she must have done something wrong for this to happen and how sorry she was. Through imagination, she began to hear him lovingly respond—*"You didn't do anything wrong Mom; it was just my time. I love you and I always will."* In that experience, Julie regained her loving connection with Jacob. She could finally remember him without feeling extreme guilt and grief. Now that she was no longer punishing herself, organic healing spontaneously occurred and she could feel joy once again.

Similarly, sixty-year-old Ted was stuck in denial two years after he was released from his job. He could not believe his employers had let him go. After all, he was a loyal and committed worker. How could this happen? Stuck in his denial, Ted was unable to find an equal position and was just getting by in a sales job with less than stellar results.

As he relaxed into his body, he saw he was fooling himself. He was fired when he had slacked off at the job because he was tired and wanted to retire, but couldn't because he needed the income. As he opened up to this inner conflict consciously during a series of three sessions, Ted realized he was wishing for something that was no longer available. Living in the past was stopping him from realistically pursuing the new job he still needed at a similar or better professional level.

Moving through his denial allowed Ted to progress through the stages of loss to acceptance almost instantly. As this realization registered in his mind and body, he got it! His interest in his current sales job changed dramatically, and he began to excel. His results and his confidence significantly improved so that he no longer wanted to retire.

At the end of an interview for a documentary, the interviewer asked: "Can I ask you a personal question? I have experienced a trauma, and I feel it is still influencing me. I can feel it right here in my chest like a ball. Is it possible for it to go away?" The tenderness in his vulnerable, young voice was touching.

"Yes, definitely," I replied, "I've witnessed thousands of people release traumatic pain. Your spirit is greater than any human experience you've had."

He broke into a big smile and his countenance transformed from tentative and anxious to light and free. It was so obvious, I asked his interview partner if she noticed anything different. When he turned to face her, she looked completely surprised and said, "Wow, you look happy."

When I asked him what had changed, he said, "I have hope," and smiled brightly and confidently. The mere shift of attention from fear to possibility can have remarkable results. Perspective is that powerful.

What sadness or grief is lingering in your body? A death, a rejection, a hurt of some kind? Close your eyes, and ask your imagination for a number between one and ten (with ten being the most) of how much sadness/grief is influencing you:

··
  1   2   3   4   5   6   7   8   9   10
··

Move your attention into your heart, and notice a word pops into your mind of what pain remains and you get a sense of what it is. Write this word down so you can work with it further in the Practice It Yourself section below.

Envy and Jealousy

Feelings of envy are extremely difficult to acknowledge because they make us feel small-minded and less than we think we should be. Thus, we rarely share these feelings with others; they are our secrets. The reality is, there's always someone out there who is more successful and others who are less successful. These "more successful" people can find others who are "more so than they" and so on. It's an almost never-ending process.

The key is for us to recognize our feelings as feedback rather than something good or bad, so we can learn from them. Jealousy is frequently a projection of what we want and feel we can't have. Looking at them as something of a Rorschach test,[9] we see in the people we envy a reflection of what is inside us that wants to express more fully. These people who inspire jealousy instead of admiration mirror a passionate purpose or inherent desire in us that wants to express in a bigger way.

At a social gathering, a woman shared how she couldn't figure out why she was feeling jealous of her friend who got a piano and was taking lessons. Finally, she realized she had always wanted to learn how to play the piano. Once she acknowledged these feelings, it happened that someone she knew was getting rid of a piano and she offered to take it. With two young children taking most of her attention, her piano lessons and practicing have become gratifying personal time.

When you allow yourself to name your jealous feelings (it takes guts), you can unabashedly uncover their hidden purpose. You also connect positively with those you envy—"*I am the same as they*"—which raises your self-esteem.

I have been blessed over the last eleven years to work with *New York Times* best-selling author Jack Canfield (classic books: *Chicken Soup for the Soul*® series and *Success Principles*™), initially as a student and progressing to coauthor and friend. There came a time when my work had expanded and grown, but remained limited compared to Jack's. I felt frustrated by reaching smaller numbers of people through RIM; I worried that many more people were needlessly suffering and I wasn't able to get to them.

Around this time, I became seriously jealous of Jack, who had always been kind and supportive to me. I saw his mastery at teaching audiences of hundreds, even thousands, of people at a time and the way he stayed authentic and honest. He could adeptly facilitate difficult seminar situations in ways that were graceful and effective. I also envied his support resources that made it easy for him to reach millions. In other words: I wanted to be him.

Initially, I felt bad that I would have these feelings for someone who was a great friend and wonderful mentor. Then I realized it wasn't about Jack; the jealous voice was from me and about me and it was saying: *"Deb, you are playing smaller than your inner urge. . . . You are playing it safe."* Sensing that truth, I decided to take more risks and step into greater visibility, and my jealousy organically dissolved. Instead of viewing Jack in comparison to me, I was able to see him as my inspiration again.

After 2008 and one of the stock market crashes, my husband and I realized we needed to limit travel for a while. When I heard our friends sharing their fun trips, I felt envious. Born an adventurer, I longed for the stimulation and excitement. The discomfort of this jealousy caused me to seek a resolution. Soon the idea of offering international retreats popped into my head. This new business venture paid for exotic travels and even brought additional income.

Not only did retreats dissolve my feelings of jealousy; they called me to expand. As I guided groups to Maui, Costa Rica, Australia, and Peru, there were constant challenges that spurred me to grow my skills, and I loved it. This growth was a springboard to greater vitality and connection.

Self Check-In

Who makes you the most jealous? What is it about this person that really gets you? Is she or he making more money? Exercising greater power? Expressing more talents? Having more fun? Fostering a healthier, fitter body? Having greater closeness in an intimate relationship? Name this quality you want more of right now. For example, I was jealous of Jack Canfield's level of successfully fulfilling his purpose in his work. Thus, I wanted to live my purpose more successfully.

Once you have named the quality you want more of, ask your imagination to give you a number on a scale of one to ten (ten being the most) of how much you are manifesting this quality currently. Whatever number pops into your mind first, receive it, letting go of any desire to edit.

| 1 | 2 | 3 | 4 | 5 | 6 | 7 | 8 | 9 | 10 |

Imagine standing in the number you received and, with eyes closed or open, looking to the "ten" where your imagination shows you an image of you speaking and acting in a way that fully embraces this quality. By looking to the "ten" from where you are, you can easily sense the step-by-step course to greater fulfillment. These steps are your road map to a more fully lived life. For example, when I looked to the "ten" level of living my purpose, I saw myself taking immediate action to write a new book, expand RIM class offerings, and seek RIM research opportunities. The underbelly of envy and jealousy is an unconscious holding back of yourself. Some of us have grown up in families and cultures feeding us messages like "Don't get too big for your britches" and "It's selfish to call attention to yourself or your needs." In these situations, you may have learned to shy away from playing at the level that excites you. The emotional result can be to think you are less capable than you are and to take fewer risks.

If this is happening for you, you can stretch beyond your comfort zone to explore. Stepping out is scary at first—until you begin to experience greater aliveness, joy, and sense of purpose. Then the call to the quest becomes compelling.

When my husband wanted to make a career change before his fiftieth birthday, we decided to put aside our work to take the kids on a yearlong personal sabbatical to Australia. Around this time, I came across a poignant quote by French philosopher André Gide: "One does not discover new lands, without losing sight of the shore for a very long time." I thought, *Oh yes, we're losing sight of the shore for a year.* That year was so transformational for the entire family, it has developed into a way of life for each of us. We have been drawn to lose sight of the shore regularly. We visit the shore of "comfortable same old" for a while, then head out again to explore unknown waters.

You have new shores calling to you, too. They are unique to your personality and talents. It is irrelevant how dramatic the risk. The important thing is to express yourself step-by-step more fully in your own way and timing.

Feelings about Feelings

What is your conditioned take on feelings? Did your family embrace feelings or judge them? Did you learn to share your feelings openly or were you shamed for feeling anger, sadness, and envy? Were you celebrated for your successes or cautioned to remain humble or silent?

It's possible to free yourself of these emotions. However, it requires you to look honestly at feelings you have judged as ugly and undesirable.

In nursing school, we learned the "dead man's test" for developing effective patient goals. If a dead man can do it, it doesn't support growth and improvement. For example, a dead man can easily accomplish the goal of not feeling angry. This phrase "if a dead man can do it" is a powerful statement emphasizing how *feeling* is a sign of life and *not feeling* is a sign of death. To allow uncomfortable feelings rather than avoid them is to be fully alive. Otherwise, we shut off the emotional faucet that also supplies joy and excitement. We think we can turn off *bad* feelings and continuously be in *good* feelings; however, the body keeps score and buried feelings eventually show up in numbness or as emotional or physical symptoms. It's interesting to notice the love-hate relationship we have with emotion. We crave the highs that enliven us and hate the lows that make us feel bad. It's no surprise we seek pleasure to avoid pain.

On the other hand, we can allow the continuous, dynamic river of feelings to flow safely regardless of how terrible they seem. There are many techniques to keep our emotional waters moving safely and evaporating naturally. Let's look at a few for you to practice.

Feelings into Words and Thoughts

When you name your feelings, it's like pouring water from a pitcher. Feelings are the water, and we are the pitchers. By expressing our deepest emotions verbally, on paper, or through movement, we pour out the feelings, see them as external to us, and regain a sense of internal spaciousness and capacity to welcome new experience. As you are learning in this book, feelings do not have to be shared with the person with whom we are upset. In fact, spilling uncensored feelings in an *imagined* way is often the most beneficial initial action. Once the intense agitation has been drained off, we can become clear about whether we need to have a real conversation. I've witnessed that most of the time it's unnecessary. Sometimes, the person with whom we are upset is elusive or unavailable. Yet we're not stuck being a victim because they aren't listening. Quite the contrary, the process happens within us, for us.

Ashley, who came in following a double mastectomy, offers a great example of how this process works. She had successfully undergone reconstructive surgery and was returning to her normal life with a supportive husband and grown children, yet she felt extremely anxious. As she closed her eyes and dipped into her body through her imagination, she saw black energy filling both of her arms where the surgery had left numbness. Although this darkness scared her, she bravely moved her attention to it, and the source of her anxiety materialized into an image of a declining self. The image looked small, bent over, weak, pale, and fragile. At the sight, Ashley's anxiety peaked—until she began to speak aloud and freely. By voicing directly to her image, she discerned a discrepancy between the image of a declining self and the truth:

You are not me. I'm not declining. I'm adapting and growing stronger each day. I won't let you scare me because you are just a shadow of a fear—a fear that's ungrounded. Wow! I feel so much better. Now, I see I was letting you haunt me as I went about my daily activities. But you aren't real. You aren't real. Thank God you aren't real.

With eyes still closed, Ashley looks over and senses that the image of the declining self has evaporated along with her anxiety.

A friend who was directly affected by the 2013 Colorado floods was feeling quite upset when tornadoes devastated her neighbors' homes again. Finally, she expressed her angst in a long, booming scream, "No." Afterwards, she noticed she felt better.

Although I had recommended uncensored writing to my psychotherapy clients, I had never tried it until I found myself in a serious power struggle with my beautiful and spirited daughter Elena when she was seven. Appropriate to her age, she resisted every request, and I felt quite inadequate. Unfortunately, being a psychotherapist did not make me invulnerable to emotional mistakes (as I secretly longed to be).

A poetry class, however, pushed me to discover the healing power of expression through spontaneous writing firsthand. I had the assignment to write about an object. Interestingly, a child's china teacup was my item, and I found myself spontaneously writing to Elena:

A tiny, rounded vessel with a hand-painted blue flower rests on a barn-wood table. The rim where lips have touched and drunk tea narrows into a leprechaun-sized handle made for small digits sticky with marmalade jelly. Fingers that search out every hole and corner hoping to find hidden treasure—old jewelry or forgotten sweets—cherished trinkets as reflected in the gleeful eye of childhood.

If only we could sit together, pouring tea and laughing. Of all that is in my care, you are most precious. Yet I let my vision wander to trivial tasks, domestic chores and half-written books. Meanwhile, my tea party chair remains vacant.

Sometimes I wish I were in someone else's body, escaping these fears. I would play trickster and tickle them from the inside out, making them giggle without knowing why. And when they were busy at work, I would make their feet itch so badly they had to get up and walk away from their obsession.

They'd never have a quiet moment because I would be there to knock at their heart, reminding them of my presence, always ready for a new joke or a reckless game. I would be so close to them that sharing the same skin wouldn't be enough; inhabiting their entire being would be my wish. The chatter and tug-of-war would tell me who I am and that I am.

Ah! Is wanting to get under my skin what your seven-year-old ego seeks? Hitting up against my resistance, you can learn your boundaries, see your ability to spar, to excite, to stir.

Little one, you own my heart, and yet I claim my body. What a mixed message that must seem. You see me as capable, full of confidence, always getting my way, juxtaposed against your childlike lack of knowing.

I, too, have childlike fears and lacks. I, too, am searching out myself amid the experiences of the world. Can you not see me as you pester me from the inside out? Of course you don't, for I don't wish it. The freedom to discover without interference is the gift I hope to offer.

I am you and you are me; how can I wrench myself out of the picture without somehow abandoning you? We come together in total union and complete conflict as you worm your way from inside me out into the light of your own separate life.

We sit together laughing and sipping tea from a small, magic teacup hand-painted with a blue flower.[10]

....

As I wrote, my hidden feelings organically materialized and connected me with Elena's playful and evolving spirit. How freeing it felt to appreciate in me the same childlike desires. My anger and guilt immediately dissolved as I vividly experienced the love-hate relationship inherent in separation. You probably guessed it already—our relationship improved the minute I lightened up.

You may remember times when you were feeling uptight, but didn't really know why until you started expressing. As your mind formulates the words, you hear yourself and gain insight. When you speak, write, or move (e.g., jogging or yoga) relative to an issue, you gain clarity and a feeling of freedom. There is no need to know the answers, to be stoic, or to control yourself—merely translate the inner experience into words as best as you can, letting go of any desire to edit.

On the other hand, the intellectual and constant retelling of a victim story becomes a broken record. Rather than releasing emotions, it deepens the groove of helplessness in the nervous system. It's easy to hear when listening to someone's story. We easily discern the tonal difference between personal release and repeating victimhood.

The good news with the RIM® process is that emotional release happens organically as long as the person is willing to explore the inner spontaneous experience.

PRACTICE IT YOURSELF

The following activities demonstrate ways you can activate a safe flow of emotion for whatever feeling/issue you wish to address. Each of these RIM practices can be applied to any emotion. For simplicity, I've assigned one of the discussed emotions of anger, sadness/grief, and jealousy to them. Feel free to mix and match in whatever order feels good to you. To go deeper, you can do all three practices successively with the same intense emotion/issue. Continue to cycle through them until you feel a significant shift. Some issues require more attention than others. Luxuriate in the time it takes—you deserve it!

Three Simple Activities to Keep Your River of Feeling Flowing

Emptying Angry Feelings through Uncensored Writing

- Arrange a quiet, personal place to sit with a pen and paper in hand.

- Write down the specific anger you identified earlier or choose another one that's bothering you.

- Put the pen to paper and begin to write whatever comes into your mind as you remember this experience. It doesn't need to make sense or look good, it can be scribbled. Pour your uncomfortable emotions onto the accepting page by writing with intensity.

- Write down whatever words come. For example, it may ramble like:

  I don't know what to say. This is stupid. I don't know. I'm so frustrated that I don't know. It feels like I don't know anything. That's what happened before, I didn't know what I wanted and I suffered. I'm so pissed about it, I can't even think.

- Continue to write whatever comes. If nothing is coming, return to this sentence lead: "What I feel as I remember this specific emotion/event is . . ."
- Take as much time and paper as needed to write yourself into a new feeling state. As you write, you leave your feelings on the paper.

Notice how this process connects you with your body and feelings. Writing allows you the unique and uncensored expression of whatever wants to be spoken. You are free to have your feelings and express them in a safe way. Giving a voice to your feelings is a necessary personal freedom. For some of us, it may be the first time we feel completely free to express what feels unspeakable.

Clearing Sadness/Grief through Your Heart

Recall the sadness/grief that showed up earlier.[11]

- Close your eyes and move your attention into your heart where *one word* pops into your mind of how you're feeling about it right now. (Take a minute.)
- As you sense this feeling, embrace it as much as you can. (Take a minute.)
- Repeat the above two actions at least two more times.

- Notice the natural dynamic nature of your feelings: how they constantly change all of their own accord without you doing anything except naming and embracing them as fully as you can.

Freeing Feelings of Envy through Movement

Now that you know the intimate relationship between your feelings and your body, you can express and process emotion physically through movement. Recall the jealous feelings that showed up earlier. Read the following simple process all the way through and then organically enact it with your eyes open or closed:

- Find a private space with enough room for you to move. (If you are doing this as a group activity, everyone's eyes are closed and there's spacing between people to allow free movement.)

- Stand up and close your eyes.

- Sense what you are feeling emotionally as you recall the specific jealous/envious feeling that showed up earlier or another emotion of your choosing. Name it in your mind or aloud.

- With background music or not, your body freely expresses this feeling physically however it wants to move. Imagine you are a kinetic art sculpture whose job is to visibly express the emotion present from moment to moment.

- Notice when your body wants to move and when it wants to remain still, when it wants to be small and when it wants to be big, when it feels strong and when it feels vulnerable . . .

- Notice how you feel in response to the spontaneous body expressions.

- Notice how your feelings are changing automatically as your body is changing positions.

- Continue to move until your body feels calmer and lighter. Sense how you're feeling now compared to when you started.

Body moves and dances—Mind speaks and listens
Heart beats and feels—Body-Mind-Heart
We are rhythms of Life

SEE & FREE

Your Feelings Have Form

Emotions are invisible, taken for granted, and dismissed much of the time, a paradox given they are some of the most powerful human forces on the planet. They inflame wars, induce death, inspire invention, and control the stock markets. Even more importantly, each of us has them—constantly!

—DEBORAH SANDELLA

When you sense the form of your feelings, you gain power over them. The importance of this learning is highlighted in Jack, Joan, and Robert's real-life outcomes.

JACK'S STORY: MOVING PAST A ROADBLOCK

Jack is an extremely smart and outgoing twenty-four-year-old. He wants to do something important in the world, but his experience in bioengineering graduate school has become a nightmare. During his two years in a doctoral program, he has sacrificed free time and self-care to conduct research. He thought the project would be perfect because it is centered on curing cancer, but he finds himself feeling depressed and alienated because there is no personal connection to helping people. Instead, he is administering mechanical tests in a solitary lab.

He feels isolated, exhausted, and knows this work does not inspire him, yet strangely he can't quite quit. Even his mother, who has a doctorate in engineering, sees this program is not a good fit with his personality and has urged him to leave. His parents are so worried about his visible decline, they offer to finance a transition to something different. Though he knows he would be happier and healthier pursuing a personal passion, it is as if he were stuck in concrete. His parents fear suicide because he seems to be on a downhill slide and unable to take action to save himself. Desperate, they arrange for him to have a phone session, since the results are just as good as in person.

Jack describes his life as miserable with little time for exercise, eating well, or friends. His school commitments permeate every aspect of his day, including sleep when he is assigned middle-of-the-night data inputs. He is so depressed that he further isolates from friends, which leaves his life reduced to work, sleep, and junk food. Still, he is immobilized and unable to speak with his supervising professor, who has a reputation for driving his students harder than anyone else in the school.

Sitting in his car on his cell phone to accommodate his research schedule, Jack begins his session by closing his eyes and gently turning his attention from the external world to an inner experience. His awareness is drawn to his Adam's apple, which appears as an orange pyramid with the point poking out through the front of his neck. As he moves his attention into the center of this pyramid to inhabit it, his imagination instantly materializes a very uncomfortable feeling of standing in choppy water. With prompting, his imagination materializes someone to calm his unease: a favorite high school teacher, Mr. Jamison, appears, and Jack immediately feels better. Finding this "good" feeling in his body, he senses warmth in his stomach.

Embracing the warmth, Jack spontaneously sees flashes of playing hockey with his friends back home. In his mind's eye, he takes off his shoes and runs up a hill laughing freely. The heaviness is gone; instead he feels weightless. His voice is transformed, and I can hear the happiness beneath his words. He rests in this exquisite experience until it feels complete.

As he looks from this current scene back to the image of himself as a graduate student he realizes:

I'm so sad I haven't been true to myself. I don't even recognize myself when I look at this person who is dead because he's given his life away to strive for something that holds no personal passion or meaning.

Sensing this sad feeling expressed in his body, Jack finds a black mass on top of his heart. As he moves his awareness into this energy, he invites an image of someone he needs to speak to—whereupon the image of Professor T, his current demanding supervisor, pops up.

With his high school teacher Mr. Jamison supporting him from just behind his right shoulder, Jack speaks:

Professor T, I never wanted to go negative on you. This research is your life, not mine. I'm not happy. I'm sad because I have spent so much time here. These years have changed me. I'm not myself here. I haven't been honest with you, and it feels good to recognize the truth now and speak it to you. Your grad students want a life outside research. You just expect us to do what you ask and give up our lives. You're not a bad person, it's just that I'm not like you. I wish you could see who I was before and how miserable I am now. I hate every minute of every day, yet I force myself to do it. And there's no opportunity to recoup. It's destroyed the things I really care about in my life, like my relationships and my health. It just doesn't work for me and I can see I need to move on.

Moving into Professor T, Jack senses his response:

Jack, I wasn't aware that you were unhappy here. I do push students too hard sometimes. I guess I'm so passionate about this research, I love every minute. I can't imagine feeling the way you do and remaining in this program. You have to do what's best for you.

Jack feels really good now and turns to Mr. Jamison to hear what he has to say. Looking out from Mr. Jamison's eyes, he senses:

Jack, it was tough. You turned away from your true self because you worried about money. Follow your heart, Jack; it's never too late. Chasing after money or fame makes you miserable. You're on earth for a reason; you'll figure it out. You have a big heart, but you focused on things that weren't you. Now you can be yourself again. I'll always be here to support you.

Jack feels strong and confident, like his best self. A few weeks later, he calls to say:

When we did that session, I thought the way my professor responded was merely what I wanted to hear, but when I actually talked to him, he said exactly that. He was understanding and sympathetic and sad to hear I'd been so unhappy without him realizing it. In fact, he said I was such a good researcher he really hated to lose me, but he couldn't imagine being so miserable in his life's work. He suggested I reap the reward of my efforts by putting in three months of summer school so I can graduate with a master's degree. I'm totally relieved. I can make it through these three months, knowing that an engineering master's will help me get a job and finance the exploring of the things I'm passionate about. It's amazing how quickly I feel hopeful again.

Jack's story reveals the power of imagination to accurately sense what's happening. Jack's imagination had revealed what the actual conversation with his teacher would be like.

JOAN'S STORY: RESTORING HEALTH BY REGENERATING PAINFUL EXPERIENCE

Joan is an attractive and quiet sixty-year-old executive assistant. She has been suffering with hepatitis C for ten years. Exposed to the illness by a blood transfusion, she feels ever more furious with the unfairness of it all. Her liver has been severely damaged, and at the time of her first session she reports her liver function tests are so abnormal, her physicians are recommending chemotherapy, a common practice at the time. Preferring to avoid chemicals, she is seeking something different.

As Joan sits on the couch, she immediately shares a litany of complaints about the bad economy, the high cost of living, and the political party in office. The mild rant of injustice rings with familiarity as if it has been her everyday habit.

When she gently closes her eyes, an imaginary journey into her body begins. Sensing her inner space as three-dimensional, she notices a strange energy around the area of her liver. She describes it as "pure blackness—all the way through"; she winces at hearing the power of her own images. As she focuses on the shape and size of this blackness, details begin to materialize: it is rough on the surface, dry and hard, solid and dense. The hard surface calls her attention most intently, and she travels deeper into it. Here she senses sticky black tar. She sounds anxious as she realizes she can't get it off—the tar is thoroughly stuck to her hands.

Joan is willing to move her awareness bravely into the stickiest part of the tar where an image of the person she needs to speak to is brought into her mind by her imagination. Much to her surprise, it's Joe, the fiancé who betrayed her twenty years earlier. They had been together for years when she discovered his affair with another woman. Joan has not engaged in another relationship.

After her imagination materializes an image of a loving guide to give her a feeling of safety, Joan begins to speak aloud directly to the image of Joe. Having tapped a previously closed well of emotion, she spontaneously finds herself saying things she has never considered, let alone spoken. The words flow like water from a pitcher:

Joe, you hurt me so badly when all I wanted to do was to love you. How could you do that to me? I wanted to be with you more than anything, and you ruined it all. . . . You ruined my life. I've never been the same. How can I trust anyone again? I can't even trust myself to choose a man. How could I have loved you so much, when you didn't give a hoot about me? I hate you! I hate what happened! I hate life where my only true love fails and I am alone.

As Joan dips further into her sorrow and voices deeper levels of rage and shame, she gradually arrives at a feeling of emptiness, and she begins to look and sound different. The lines around her eyes that make her look older relax, and the color of her complexion brightens. She begins to speak with a self-aware voice:

I should never have trusted you, Joe. Years before your affair, I noticed how you looked at my sister. You flirted with all the girls. I guess I was so flattered you chose to be with me, I turned a blind eye to the kind of guy you really were. You were a womanizer from the beginning. If I had it to do over, I'd break up with you the first time you were disrespectful to me by ogling another girl while I sat next to you. I would tell you in no uncertain terms, Joe, I refuse to stand for this kind of disregard. I deserve better. I am leaving you.

Joan's voice is transformed from helpless and frustrated to independent and strong. She has released the stuck memory of Joe and succeeded in standing in her power. As she turns her attention to her body, she sees the black tar in her liver is gone. Though her eyes remain closed, she describes feeling "relieved" and smiles. Searching for this new energy of relief in her body, there's a bright white light in the center of her chest. Immersing herself in it, she feels unweighed down, calm, and happy. These good feelings are visceral, and she leaves feeling changed.

Over the next year, Joan comes in seven more times and again ventures into her body to uncover deeper previously unrecognized issues. Her attention is drawn consistently to her liver, where a new quality presents itself. Once she senses her liver filled with heavy red energy, another time with jagged glass. Each time, mining her body for details takes her into deeply felt pent-up anger and rage. During one session, she travels to her teen years, where she undergoes surgery for scoliosis and is hospitalized, immobilized for many weeks. Even more excruciating is the reality that her family rarely visits.

Joan keeps rewinding her life further back in time with each session until eventually a toddler appears. Looking through her vulnerable three-year-old eyes, she sees her older sister as the parental favorite, with little Joan feeling unloved. In the innocence of childhood, "little Joan" assumes she is "less than" her sister and "not good enough." As her adult self supports the little girl to speak, her parents listen and tearfully apologize for their unintentional ignorance. She finally feels seen and heard by them, and her perceived history changes from the inside. She feels the reality of being loved all along; it was all a misunderstanding. As Joan has a physical experience of feeling loved by her parents, the old unloved belief dissolves like magic. After a year and eight sessions, Joan strides into the office beaming to share:

> Guess what! The results of my liver function tests are NORMAL! I see now I was holding all that anger in my liver. Isn't that strange? I didn't know I was doing it at the time, yet I was. I feel so different. My body is so much lighter and brighter. I am now a woman who believes she deserves to have what she wants—I own my feelings and speak honestly. I am so happy.

Joan's story demonstrates how processing one's past emotional life is intimately related to health and vitality. She suffered for ten years with hepatitis C, but after eight sessions over a year the illness remitted.

ROBERT'S STORY: DISARMING HIDDEN FEARS BOOSTS FINANCIAL SUCCESS

Robert is an entrepreneur who started his own company a few years ago. He's previously been extremely successful as a manufacturing consultant. He has a knack for walking into factories and immediately seeing where a kink in the flow is creating inefficiency. Now on his own, he's struggling to attract a consistent stream of clients. As a solitary businessperson, he recognizes he must balance courting new clients and providing services to current clients. Constantly struggling to maintain cash flow, he's always tired.

Robert seeks a session because a large manufacturing company is considering a long-term contract for his services, and he is anxious to broker a deal. After all, it would solve his cash flow problems; it would also provide stable income and time to court other clients. Robert nervously feels his business future is hanging on signing this client, and he wants success.

As he closes his eyes, his attention is drawn to his left thigh muscle, which appears yellow in his imagination. Inside his thigh, the muscle seems solid and heavy. The surface is like armor with a shiny stainless steel surface. Moving his attention into the armor, he senses:

It's protection . . . the protection I needed when I was vice president of operations in my last job. I clashed with the boss and was fired. The politics resulted in some heavy-handed action that made me very angry.

Finding the anger in his body, Robert senses a pyramid in his throat. The surface of it is smooth with etched blocks and a cold temperature. As he moves into the cold, the person he needs to speak to appears. Unexpectedly, it's his mom who died less than a year earlier. He tells her:

Mom, I know you understand me. I think you knew I hoped to get canned so I could get a severance. I was desperate to get out on my own and have control. Afterwards, the clients lined up, and it was my big opportunity. Otherwise I might not have done it. I'm feeling really good, Mom, about this new potential opportunity to earn big money. You've never understood my feelings about finances, and I think you judged me as being driven by money. Sometimes, I even worry I'm being selfish because I'm focused on the money. Because of this, I've felt I needed to be cautious around you and Dad. As I say it aloud, it feels silly for me to worry about what you think or how you perceive me. Yet, I am concerned how you might judge me—that I am coming from greed rather than service. I feel restricted . . .

As I speak that aloud, I can feel you are understanding me and apologizing.

Shifting attention over into his mom looking at Robert, he senses and speaks for her:

Wow! I'm so glad you shared. I know who you are and that the world deserves you and your talents. Let go of any expectations you've perceived from Dad and me. We're following you and learning from you. I'm always here for you. I'll always be here. You'll always be my little boy. I know how strong you have been for your sibs and Dad after my passing. You're doing a great job as a parent and husband.

As he receives his mom's expressions like a stream of colored energy, a jet of white light fills Robert and he describes feeling "power and mastery." Looking for the location of this feeling in his body, he finds it in his right bicep, which is curled up like a muscle man pose. There in his muscle is the blue logo of his company and beneath it is gold bullion stacked like Fort Knox. Happily moving his attention into it, he senses gold penetrating every cell in his body creating a "nice body buzz." The gold radiates from his body into the space around him.

A month later, Robert shares that the client successfully signed on; he is thrilled to be on his way to creating a stable and profitable business. A year later, his company is booming. Robert demonstrates how hidden feelings influence us in seemingly unrelated ways.

HOW IT WORKS—PRACTICALLY AND SCIENTIFICALLY

Descartes argued in the seventeenth century that human beings are distinct from other animals because of the ability to *think*. He called attention to our self-awareness while in thought, which reflects a higher level of evolution. His famous statement, "I think, therefore I am," became the foundation for contemporary Western thought and rooted a cultural belief that to think and analyze makes us superior.

In contrast to *thinking, feeling* is invisible and elusive. Absent apparent substance, feelings can seem unbounded, out of control, and overwhelming. They completely frustrate the analytic left brain, which loves to measure and solve problems. The intellect has difficulty controlling what is unseen and unpredictable.

Freud's discovery of the unconscious contributed immensely to our understanding of ourselves as human beings. On the other hand, his theory stigmatized our hidden feelings as abnormal and diagnosable as illness. He wrote extensively about the contents of the unconscious as destructive and forbidden desires that result in psychological and psychosomatic symptoms.

It is no surprise we are often suspicious and untrusting of our feelings and want to control them. Western culture values the qualities of levelheadedness, logic, and nonemotionality. We tend to operate as though our analytic skills keep us safe and our emotions get us into trouble. This tendency often shows up in clients who have a history of abuse as the desire to micromanage the details of their immediate physical environments to create a feeling of safety. We have come to value thinking over feeling.

In reality, both thinking and feeling provide vitally important feedback to support our survival and help us flourish. Bias toward thinking leads to a depreciation of emotion as a core resource, and the intelligence of emotion is often feared and ignored rather than used effectively.

Chapter one explained how feelings are part of an emotional feedback system, keeping us safe in an unpredictable world. Rather than being a handicap, the expression of emotion offers a natural, internal compass that the thinking brain often ignores. The language of feelings, however, is not linear, logical, and verbal like the language of thinking. The way the emotional brain learns is different from the process of the rational brain. In this book, you are learning how to decode the language of feelings to understand how they work and to use them in beneficial ways.

Similar to how our physical body heals naturally by regenerating tissue, our feelings function to develop insight, direction, and resourcefulness. As we understand and use our emotions effectively, we significantly increase our resilience and ability to navigate the full range of life experiences, including hurt, trauma, and catastrophic events.

One of the secrets to understanding the intelligence of our emotions is to *see* and *sense* their form as we do with physical feedback. For instance, when we see it snowing outside and read the thermometer, we easily identify current conditions and choose to dress appropriately. We've heard stories of climbers whose perceptual feedback systems became compromised because of altitude and cold, and they were at risk because they weren't cognizant of dangerous weather conditions. Disconnected from their normal internal feedback, they removed clothes at high altitude and died of exposure.

Feedback from our feelings can be elusive. Even excruciating emotional pain does not show up externally as a bruise or a cut or bleeding. Knowing what will help or harm us in the physical world is a lot clearer than sensing what will help or harm us in our emotional world.

The most common way we manage feelings is to talk about them. Sharing our feelings with another has many benefits, including interpersonal support, connection, and ventilation. Yet we are using a primarily analytic, thinking function in response to an emotional problem. Talking *about* feelings transitions us away from *feeling* them and into *thinking*, where we are removed from the immediate site of injury—the cellular/gut/experiential level of what originally occurred. As with physical wounds, healing is needed at the site of origin. You don't put a cast on your arm when you have a broken leg!

But don't worry! Your emotional feedback system is designed more perfectly than the best computer and as quick as Google. It offers an adept and effective interpreter to communicate the form of feelings to your intellect, so you can be confident in understanding and using emotion effectively. Guess what it is? It's not a tool, book, expert, or anything external. It's right inside you, and everyone has it: *imagination*—clever, insightful, unattached to ideology or politics, and able to synthesize data from everywhere including your head, heart/body, and spirit to create solutions. In other words, imagination is magical and practical at the same time! As the poet Ted Hughes once remarked: "Imagination isn't merely a surplus mental department meant for entertainment, but the most essential piece of machinery we have if we are going to live the lives of human beings."

Imagination is the readily available, no-cost communicator that translates emotion into form for the mind to comprehend and use. Imagination spontaneously unfolds the *form* of feelings for your mind to grasp; the logical head is compelled to follow these quantifiable clues because it is good at deciphering codes, and it loves to find answers and win the game!

As we appreciate our feelings, we naturally build on Descartes' "I think, therefore I am," to realize "I feel, therefore I am more than I think." Bringing together the resources of head and heart, we understand we are more than our human thoughts and feelings. There is something in us that is so much more than our human condition, yet it is hard to put into words. It is the inner feeling you've had since you were a child . . . the feeling of being special . . . the feeling of being born for a reason (even if you do not know what it is), which, at the risk of sounding arrogant, you may not talk about and may even forget. This same awareness intuitively senses the purity and innocence of babies, the profundity of love, and the indescribable beauty of nature. It creates warm feelings in your body when you hold hands with someone you love, and it senses something greater when you look in the eyes of another human being and see that person's soul. For the sake of simplicity, we will call it human spirit, the intelligence of life itself that expresses as pure awareness and the interconnectedness of all things.

Now head, heart, and spirit have come together with the mutual goal of discovering the root cause of a problem in your mind or body. They travel together as a caravan of unlikely partners distinctly unique from each other, each with a specific role and talent. The *head* is in charge of thinking; the *heart* is in charge of feeling; and the *spirit* realizes the creative, infinitely thriving power of life while *imagination* acts as translator and synthesizer.

Like detectives, this group hunts down culprits by registering each sensory clue through colors, shapes, sizes, sounds, textures, smells, temperatures, weights, densities, feelings, and urges. Step-by-step, the excitement builds and the tension grows as they close in on the suspect in the same ways displayed by Jack, Joan, and Robert and all the others through their stories. As if playing a game of Clue, they want to discover who did what, where, and how.

By the time this improbable crew successfully unearths the root cause of what is creating a problem in the system, they are deeply unified. They form a supportive and affectionate consortium with triple powers. All share an attitude of destined success and an immense awareness of bravery and courage as they stand together to defeat any enemy. *There is no more feeling alone!*

Who is the culprit, you ask? An astute question! The unknown and unseen culprit hides in the shadows of the subconscious. Since we have been primed to think of the subconscious as a closet of monsters to be avoided, we tend to fear it. Thus, we avoid the unconscious storage room where the creative solution is hidden.

Freud discovered that thoughts, feelings, beliefs, and memories in the subconscious are free to create havoc because they run without supervision from the conscious, intellectual mind. Like a misbehaving adolescent who sneaks out of the house without parental consent, unseen thoughts and feelings are free to seek immediate gratification to numb discomfort without regard for consequences; they abdicate accountability—because that is the job of the conscious mind, right? Like the parent of a teen acting out, each of us suffers the stress of being responsible for what our subconscious creates without our agreement; we suffer the unexplained results of broken relationships, extra pounds, lack of performance, accidents, and illnesses. And we wonder why our lives are not working—because the conscious mind is doing everything it *knows* to be successful. It is the *unknown* subconscious thoughts and feelings working in the background that end up as our culprit—who would have thunk it? We are hunting the shadows of ourselves.

Carl Jung discovered the primary language of the unconscious to be symbolic. Clearly, the unconscious speaks in graphic, sensorial, experiential, metaphorical, and feeling messages. When I first learned to use the computer, I had to learn to speak its language. It was frustrating to execute a simple task without a language the computer could understand. My usual way of verbalizing a request definitely didn't work. Just like the computer, the unconscious has no evil desire to trick or hide from us; rather its capacity is limited to communicating through its own language, which is foreign to rational structures. Fortunately and naturally, imagination is adept at the unconscious language; it loves to express in graphic, sensorial, and metaphorical ways. The good news is our imagination is constantly available to translate issues and answers instantly into informative images, thoughts, memories, and feelings.

As we use imagination to communicate with all the aspects of ourselves, we open a portal to the unconscious in an intelligent and understandable way. For example, to hear the word *soft* is a primarily intellectual, verbal communication. But if you're given something *soft* to touch, you understand at a gut, sensory level. You do not need a description of what *soft* is; you actually have your own physical experience. If asked to recall a time you felt *softness* in a *lovely* way, your imagination seeks both a memory of a soft texture and an emotional feeling of lovely.

The memory you tap eventually tracks a specific past event. You have elicited the sensory experience of *soft* and the emotional experience of *lovely*. What if you find the memory of *soft* that has popped into your mind actually was not *lovely*, it was *stressful*. Your imagination has accessed something in your subconscious that seeks to be known or else it would not pop up. After working closely with the subconscious and imagination for over forty years, I have found that they consistently bring up exquisitely purposeful images. In other words, this stressful memory has shown up because it is ready to be liberated from the dark shadows out into the light of recognition and to be released for a beneficial yet unknown purpose. When you learn how to harvest these revelations, they lose their ability to harm you.

You can ask your imagination simply to translate where in your body this *stressful* feeling is. As you sense it in your chest, your gut, or elsewhere, its shape, color, size begin to formulate. Maybe it is a ball or a cube or an amorphous energy that is yellow or red or dark. It may move as a wave, a vibration, or stillness. The meaning of the form created by your imagination is unimportant. What is vital is that it has become visible to the head and felt by the heart. As we sense the form of feelings, they gain boundaries and become more manageable. They are contained to a specific area and size instead of seeming overwhelming and out of control. Thus, the head is encouraged and empowered.

Notice how compelling it was for Jack, Joan, and Robert to tune in to their spontaneous multisensory experiences. You have that same natural ability to sense and describe the thoughts, feelings, and images that arise spontaneously through your imagination. Neurons in your brain and body light up and locate the source of the problem. You access something within you that seeks to be known, although your thinking mind may be unaware of it. How right it feels to have imagination effortlessly reveal the problem and the solution.

Although this process may sound complicated, it's actually quite simple—almost childlike. In fact, children engage in the process more easily than adults. The golden secret Freud overlooked is that hidden blocks and their antidotes lie in the same uncharted areas of the unconscious. They are readily available when you ask your imagination to translate. Once there is a measurable path to follow, your head, heart, and spirit walk together through your body to healing.

When you use your imagination, it is a bit like putting on night-vision goggles to see forms in the shadows of your head, heart, and spirit. Emotion is perceived as *energy* and quantified by size, shape, color, texture, temperature, weight, and other details. Sometimes the form becomes specific, such as a belt so tightly buckled around the waist the person cannot breathe fully or a binding band across the forehead, causing pain. This sensation is compelling and intensely felt. Although it likely holds specific symbolism, the meaning is irrelevant, unlike in other psychologically oriented techniques. What is important is how you are guided deeper into a personal connection with your inner self. You are gently dipping into your psyche without thinking; it is similar to being engrossed in a spellbinding movie or novel. This captivation tricks your intellectual defenses and leaves open the door to the unconscious to regenerate positive outcomes; it feels like a vivid dream, except in this dream you can transform scary images.

The Form of Feelings

The form of feelings is symbolic and sensorial. Thus, tuning in to imagination allows whatever emotion is alive in you to be known. As your feelings change, a shift in their form automatically shows up as a concrete image for your logical head to grab hold of. Below are some common images that demonstrate how the symbolic language of feelings registers a dramatic healthy shift:

Heavy vs. Light

Have you noticed how some emotions feel *heavy*? In fact, this is how we conversationally describe tense situations. "That was heavy," people say of difficult experiences. The energy of unresolved feelings appears to have weight that can make it seem like we are carrying a burden both physically and metaphorically. When imagination graphically captures the essence of the weight of an issue or conflict, the intellect begins to take it seriously and give it attention. Having the virtual feeling of growing lighter creates relief and freedom. We sense a physical unburdening because we have actively *let go of* outdated fears, pain, and anxieties. Imagination easily quantifies this change when we ask for a number that represents the weight of this emotion before and after an experience. The number that spontaneously pops into our minds allows us to register the shift.

After this type of work, the most common comment I hear is "I feel different and lighter." People look physically brighter and younger. A client who had scheduled a RIM process for other family members laughingly said, "After my husband's process, he looks ten years younger, and after my teenage son's work, he looks three years more mature. I'm delighted with both!"

Emotional heaviness sometimes shows up as actual body weight. Liz, a middle-aged mother, had been working enthusiastically to take off extra weight through diet and regular exercise.

Although she lost weight initially, she hit a plateau. Without changing her diet or exercise habits, she eventually lost thirty more pounds as she engaged in a series of RIM experiences and shed years of buried anger with her parents. At the end of each process, she remarked, "I feel lighter and lighter."

Empty vs. Full

Feelings of emptiness can be symbolized as a hole that cannot be filled. Metaphorically, this shows up when there is a sense of not receiving emotional nourishment as a child as a bottomless pit visible in the torso—there can never be enough. To talk about this feeling is one thing; however, to actually sense a gaping hole in your chest significantly raises the level of intensity. Fear and anxiety quickly rise, which localizes the feeling of *emptiness* in the body. By tracking the fear and anxiety, the energy block can be embraced and loosened. A dramatic emotional shift happens when the client senses the *bottom* of the hole and brings in virtual support. The logical mind, frustrated with what is unknown and invisible, is relieved when it graphically sees an identifiable problem, no matter how difficult it first appears. When the head sees there is a bottom, anxiety dissolves and it immediately mobilizes to find a way to the top. To hit bottom and survive is mobilizing!

Alice's feelings had formed a hole in her chest. As she and her imagined safety figure reached the bottom of the hole and she was given permission to do what she wanted, she said, "I want to scream" as she let out a high-pitched sound. When asked what was happening, she said, "I am growing bigger and the hole doesn't seem so deep." After shouting to her husband in the other room that she was okay (we were on Skype so she was in her bedroom at home), Alice let go of restraint and screamed at the top of her lungs for five or six shouts until she eventually started laughing spontaneously. As we laughed together, she shared, "I am full-size and out of the pit; it feels really good." Alice had allowed the traumatic feeling, gone into it, and liberated herself from the helplessness of being stuck in a deep well. She later reported this feeling of personal power helped her heal two large fibroid tumors with visualization.

Loved vs. Unloved

A feeling of being alone and unloved is another common culprit hiding in the subconscious. The innocent child in us feels forgotten and abandoned because our parents or a significant other didn't adequately meet our needs for safety and love. A natural feeling arises that if we understand how something happened, we can prevent it from happening again, so we make up a story based on incomplete data and immature logic. Down deep, we frequently blame ourselves for the failure—a belief we are "not enough," "undeserving," or "less than."

The fact is, no matter how much someone loves us, because they are human, they are susceptible to meeting their instinctive needs first, getting angry, leaving emotionally/physically, and sometimes dying. They cannot fulfill our existential need for absolute love and acceptance—our desire for a 100 percent guarantee!

How wonderful that relief can be available quickly and easily at a virtual level. Imagination can materialize powerful and loving resources for the child who felt abandoned and alone. As a visceral experience, being loved is unquestioned because it registers in the body as a gut feeling, as you saw in Joan's story, which supported her liver function test returning to normal.

Your imagination, like an advanced Google search, finds the exquisitely perfect figure to be a virtual resource. In the same way forgotten emotions materialize, hidden resources also rise into awareness. The intuitive imagination chooses perfectly, as you have seen in the stories described earlier. For example, Jack immediately feels strong when his favorite high school teacher appears; Joan is able to acknowledge and say things she's never considered once she is supported by a guardian angel;

and Robert's deceased mom helps him get to the bottom of his financial block.

Symbolic Images

Imagination has an amazing ability to access disparate thoughts, feelings, and memories in the reservoir of the mind, heart, and spirit and instantly formulate insightful, metaphoric, and meaningful images. The term *visualization* is misleading because imagination is not limited to vision. Rather, imagining evokes a multisensory experience. Visual, auditory, and kinesthetic ways of processing information are used. Although each of us has a dominant style, we can access all three. For example, someone who is a primary visual learner tends to see pictures, while a person who is an auditory learner hears voices and sounds. The kinesthetic learner is very sensitive to touch, sensations, and feelings. All of these channels are equally successful in sensing the form of feelings, and with practice, they become stronger. Dr. Audrey Boxwell studied the practice of inner sensing and found four weeks of repeated use significantly increases the strength of the messages.[1]

The astuteness of spontaneous images, memories, thoughts, and feelings to resolve specific conflicts is stunning. In preparation for a surgery, college-age Shawna seems confident and unconcerned as she enters the office. However, her process reveals different feelings just beneath the surface. When her imagination is asked for an image that represents her upcoming surgery, Shawna spontaneously senses a vision of herself standing on the banks of a large lake with stormy, crashing waves. "I must get to the other side to survive and I'm afraid I can't make it," she says as she begins to cry. Intense fear reflects on her face and in her voice. As we call in a caring and powerful virtual resource to help, an image of Shawna's cousin Linda pops into her awareness. In real life, Linda was hit and killed by an out-of-control, elderly driver while volunteering on a highway cleanup crew just a few months earlier. No doubt, her cousin's shocking death is the source of Shawna's intense fear of going under anesthesia. However, we do not talk about it because that would be engaging at the head level. Instead we move into Shawna's heart, and she speaks directly to Linda:

> It is so unfair, you never had a chance. He ran you over like you were thrown-away trash on the side of the highway. I'm so sad and I feel so helpless. There was nothing you could do and there's nothing I can do now; it hurts so bad. I can't understand it. My faith in people and being able to control what happens to me is destroyed. It was obliterated in that moment. How can I go on knowing someone can die at any time when they haven't done anything wrong; in fact, you were doing a good deed.

Sensing Linda's response, Shawna hears a perspective not voiced prior to her death:

> Shawna, I understand your feelings. Yes, it was unfair and I had no control. You are right, it was a shock. What I know now, Shawna, is I am happier than I've ever been. I am free. I love you, Shawna, and I don't want you to suffer; I'm not suffering. It was my time and that driver just happened to be there. I have no regrets, and I want to support you now. You are a good person. I always admired you. Your surgery is going to be fine, and I'll help you cross the lake. It will be easy and natural. Come, let's go.

Shawna, with Linda by her side, jumps into the lake and swims across easily. As she pulls herself wet and chilly onto the opposite bank, she also feels victorious and confident. Two days later, Shawna goes under anesthesia with a feeling of peace, and her surgery is successful.

The way Shawna's imagination managed all the interconnected issues was amazing to witness. As each issue spontaneously popped into her awareness, it proved perfect. First,

Shawna had no idea her cousin's death was causing her to be afraid of dying during surgery. As she hears Linda's eloquent reply, she begins to feel more empowered by the sensation of having Linda's support with her.

Second, Shawna's fear of surviving surgery, which is symbolized in the challenge to swim the stormy lake, is resolved through the experience of making it successfully across accompanied by Linda; there is no more feeling alone. Shawna viscerally lived the experience through imagination. Rather than intellectual discussions about her upcoming surgery, she experienced healing in the *fault line* at the source of her fear.

Similarly, Shawna's emotionally felt experience of Linda as a support is powerful and soothing regardless of what her intellectual mind believes true or possible. Rather, it becomes a treasured memory.

Georgia, a retired teacher who planned to marry and share her inherited farm with her boyfriend, was unsure of her decision. She was concerned her dad, who willed the farm to her upon his passing, would not like the idea. In a brief process, we asked her imagination to show a video of what it would look like to live this choice. As she quietly watched, she suddenly voiced with a frightened gasp: "Oh my! I can see this is a bad choice. No, I will not include him on the deed."

Next, we ask her imagination to create a new movie that responds to her alarm. As she watches, she sees her boyfriend move in and live with her without financial ownership of the farm. After sensing these profound images, she feels confident she must change her legal decision to share the farm rather than risk an outcome with which she cannot live. The confusion and ambivalence are gone.

You have an extraordinary capacity to recognize your wisdom about any issue, problem, or decision by asking your imagination to locate where in the body this issue/question resides, creating an image of the root cause, and bringing in virtual resources for safety. The issue then resolves organically.

The Emotional Benefits of Daydreaming

Are you wondering what science has to say? Our naive ability for sensing the form of feelings employs a nonlogical, free-flowing state of mind similar to daydreaming and night dreaming. Daydreaming or mind wandering has been found by some estimates to be happening 50 percent of the time for most of us. In today's science, it's seen as healthy drifting that allows us to be creative and plan for the future by imagining different events. Scientist Richard Fisher suggests: "If a person's mind is wandering, they outperform their peers in a range of tasks where flashes of insight are important, from imaginative word games to exercises in original thinking and invention."[2]

Fisher suggests the reason we sometimes zone out in daydreaming is to think creatively beyond the rigid limits imposed by the executive control in the brain. Similarly, engaging the mind in sensing the form of feelings disengages the brain's logic filter and allows an uncensored process to commence.

Further research finds unidentified, disparate concepts spontaneously link in new ways during daydreaming. In one experiment led by Benjamin Baird at the University of California, Santa Barbara, volunteers spent two minutes listing unusual ways to use a brick. Afterward, some were assigned a mindless task and others given a test that required their complete attention. As expected, people doing the mindless task drifted off significantly more than the others. When both groups were asked to return to the original creative task, the group whose minds had wandered came up with 40 percent more answers while the focused group barely improved.[3]

There is also some indication that daydreaming is associated with success in creative ventures. In a small 2003 study by Shelley Carson at Harvard University, people who had written a published novel, patented an invention, or had an art show at a gallery displayed more mind wandering than the average person.[4] The opposite of mind drifting is the focused mind in intense anxiety. Research shows concentration on negative, anxious thoughts interrupts creative problem-solving.[5]

Researcher Malia Mason has located the area of the brain that is activated during these free-flowing wanderings through functional MRI; it is a constellation of neural regions across the brain known collectively as the default network.[6] What is curious is that the unfocused mind was found by Kalina Christoff and colleagues at the University of British Columbia to activate some parts of the brain associated with the executive control functions. They suggest this activity is not full-blown concentrated thinking, but the ability to record and remember important ideas floating into awareness during or immediately after daydreaming.[7] In other words, the functions of the logical mind activated during daydreaming create an operating system that allows the content to be understood and retained, yet remain free from the limits of logic. This finding supports the organic nature of emotion presented in this book. When we sense the form of our feelings as described in this chapter, we disengage the thinking mind enough to allow imagination to bring together old and new images in an innovative, beneficial way.

Nighttime dreaming also displays similarities to the non-thinking state of mind employed when you sense the form of your feelings as described above. For example, sleep researcher Rosalind Cartwright defines dreaming as "a sensory experience, mostly visual but with other senses involved, connected by a narrative structure that we believe to be real at the time, no matter how bizarre." This definition fits quite well with the experiences of Jack, Joan, and Robert described earlier.[8] The difference, of course, is that these people were awake and knew they were in a dreamlike state. In both nighttime dreaming and the above client experiences, the intellect provides the operating system for you to understand what is happening, yet what unfolds seems to have a life of its own without the filter of logical thinking. You've probably had at least one experience of waking up crying, laughing, or sweating because of a dream. In the same way, when you are sensing the form of feelings, the experience is so real it elicits an intense emotional and physical response. The good news is you are awake and can regenerate happy endings. The new self-affirming outcomes are felt intensely and stored as visceral experiences.

Contemporary thinking emphasizes dreams as being about emotion or affect. In her sleep lab, when Rosalind Cartwright studied people undergoing divorce, she found normal dreaming consistently improves mood unless the sleeper is clinically depressed. Dreams that modulated mood were ones where the ex-spouse was in the dream and intense emotion was felt and expressed to them.[9]

She suggests dreaming melds new and old memory fragments to modify the network of how the emotional self conceives of "*Who am I? What is good for me and what is not?*" She goes on to say: "In this way, dreaming diffuses the emotional charge of the event and so prepares the sleeper to wake ready to see things in a more positive light, to make a fresh start."[10] This sounds quite similar to the client outcomes you've read above.

In other words, day and night dreaming are both emotionally beneficial. Brain research also supports a similarity between the effects of day and night dreams. Researcher at the University of California, Santa Cruz, William Domhoff builds on evidence from brain lesions and neuroimaging to argue that the part of the brain that supports night dreaming may be a subsection of the same constellation in the brain active during daydreaming and simulation.[11] Domhoff suggests both nighttime dreams and daydreams revolve around current concerns, regrets, unfinished intentions, and hopes for the future. Both are likely to call up negative situations, although daydreams are generally more pleasant, more satisfactory in outcome, and more transparent in meaning because people feel more in control.[12]

PRACTICE IT YOURSELF

Now you get to practice how to sense the form of your feelings. Start with connecting your thinking head with your feeling heart. All you have to do is 1) close your eyes and 2) control your breathing.

Closing Your Eyes

Closing your eyes instantly interrupts the influx of external visual data. As the brain gives up looking for visual cues, attention turns inward to sense the virtual world of sensation. Sleep is the extreme demonstration of this process. At bedtime, we close our eyes and feel our dreams as viscerally real. Some of our nighttime experiences will be remembered the next day and some will not. It is not uncommon for our dreams to seem more intensely real than our daily life experience because the mind's logic filter that determines what is real is turned off. There is a fully felt emotional experience without interpretation or distancing by the intellect, so anything can happen and be felt as true.

Controlling Your Breath

When autonomic body activities (body functions that automatically occur without conscious thought, such as breathing) are manually induced, a bridge is created between head and heart, mind and body.

For centuries, controlling the breath has been utilized by some cultures to expand mind and body awareness. Yogic rituals in ancient India used secret breathing practices to tame the body and raise conscious awareness. In earliest Egypt, specific breathing patterns were used during orgasm to increase vibrancy and elevate one's self-awareness. The Chinese ancient healing practice of qigong begins with practicing deeper, slower, controlled breathing. Contemporary yoga practices also focus on deeper breathing in conjunction with poses. Drawing in air by using the lower abdominal muscles rather than the upper chest is a common characteristic in many of these breathing practices.

By merely closing your eyes, you easily disconnect the main viewfinder of the brain and turn your attention inward. Further, by controlling your usually autonomic breath, your head becomes intently focused on inner sensing instead of analysis. Expanding your belly with each inhale will further divert your attention from the external environment.

Now that you're ready to connect head and heart, read each of the following paragraphs one by one. Close your eyes and practice the described activity before you proceed to the next. Once you've made your way through all of them, you can turn to the abbreviated Sensing the Form of Feelings activity box to practice the total process.

Sensing the Form of Feelings Activities

In the same way the people in our example stories were guided, you'll be guided through a simple personal process to *sense the form of your feelings.* Although it may not be a familiar practice, you can't do it wrong. It's all about merely becoming aware of how it feels to look inward rather than outward.

Conscious Seeing

- With your eyes open, look at something in your current view and notice the physical details of its appearance. When you focus your attention on the colors, textures, and shapes, it becomes clearer. For example, if you are looking at a tree, you notice the varying textures and depths of the bark, the shapes of leaves, and their variegated colors. If you are looking at the sky, you notice the general shape and speed of passing clouds and the images contained in the cloud patterns. If you are looking at an object, you take note of its specific size and location in comparison to things around it. Sensing how color and light influence the appearance of the object and give it depth, notice if there are moving parts and their pattern and speed.

• With your eyes open, expand your attention to include your accompanying thoughts and feelings. Notice if there's curiosity, surprise, awe, calm, excitement, restlessness. Whatever shows up is perfect.

Closed Eye Sensing

• When you're ready, gently close your eyes. Notice your first reaction. It may be awareness of how the natural light comes in through your eyelids to form shadows, or extraneous thoughts, or maybe impatience to get on with the activity? Whatever your response, welcome it.

• With closed eyes, focus on your breathing and notice the exact point where your breath comes in and the precise point where it starts to flow out.

• Noticing whether your inhale is longer, shorter, or the same as your exhale, take control of your breathing, and make your inhale longer than your exhale for three or four breaths.

• Now reverse the pattern and make your exhale longer than your inhale for three or four breaths. Notice the varying body sensations.

• Taking a deep cleansing breath, notice how far down in your body your breath usually settles, and on the next breath go deeper. Imagine your inhale passing down through your lungs, your navel, and even all the way down to your toes, and sense how the air naturally rises back up through your navel, your lungs, and out your nose.

Conscious Body Seeing

- As you explore the inside of your body with closed eyes, allow your attention to go to your left foot. Fully aware of your left foot, notice the feeling of your left foot against the surface beneath it.

- As your attention focuses on your left foot, your awareness easily spreads from your big toe to your second, third, fourth, and baby toes.

- Now that your left foot is lit up with your attention, notice your right foot. Spreading your attention to your right foot, become aware of your right foot as you did with the left and notice how it wakes up.

Conscious Body Energy Sensing

- Easily moving your awareness into the center of your body, sense it in all its dimensions. Notice whatever calls your attention first, and embrace whatever shows up.

- Sensing this energy, notice the form your imagination is giving it: the color and texture of the energy, whether it is rough or smooth, and how much space it occupies in your body. Is this energy just under your skin or does it go all the way through your spine? Sense the form and movement of this energy as best as you can and notice if it looks like a specific object. Take as much time as you need.

Conscious Moving into the Energy

- As you observe this energy, imagine moving your attention into the center of it as best as you can. Rest in it.

Receiving Whatever Thoughts, Feelings, and Images Arise

- As you rest in this place, receive whatever arrives: spontaneous thoughts, feelings, and images are sensed easily, and you notice how it feels. Take as much time as you need or want.

- Sit in this space until it feels complete or as long as you want. As you rest here, your mind reveals what you have learned through this process.

Anchor your experience by recording your insights. I recommend getting a new blank book or opening a new file on your computer for recording the insights you will gather in this book:

MY PERSONAL INSIGHTS

What I noticed . . .

What surprised me . . .

What didn't surprise me . . .

What I sensed when my attention moved into the energy . . .

How I feel now . . .

What I learned that I didn't know before . . .

Previous learning of which I am reminded . . .

You can go to the Sensing the Form of Feelings activity box on p. 69 and easily practice the total process.

Congratulations! You have sensed the form of your feelings. Your unconscious may want to reveal only so much at this time. Research finds that practicing twice a week for at least four weeks significantly improves one's receptivity, so stay with it and you'll get deeper relaxation and more expansive insights as you go.[13] You will become more and more aware of the form of your feelings so you can reshape them in self-affirming ways.

My feelings are intelligent, directive, and revealing
From the inside out they rise, flow, reveal
Uncovering, releasing, freeing
Reshaping my experience
Lifting my mood

SENSING THE FORM OF FEELINGS

- *Gently closing your eyes, you notice your first reaction. . . .*

- *Your attention turns to recognizing when your breath comes in and then starts to flow out of your body.*

- *Making your inhale longer than your exhale for three or four breaths, notice how this feels.*

- *Reversing it, make your exhale longer than your inhale for three or four breaths.*

- *With your attention on your left foot, become aware of your big toe down to your baby toe.*

- *Noticing your right foot, share your attention with it and notice how it responds.*

- *Easily moving your awareness into the center of your body, notice what calls your attention.*

- *Giving your full attention to it, notice its size, shape, and color.*

- *Notice the texture—rough or smooth, wet or dry, under your skin or deep into your body.*

- *Moving your attention into the center of it, embrace it as much as you can.*

- *Spontaneous thoughts, feelings, and images arise and you sense them easily.*

- *Receive whatever comes: welcome it, allow it, and embrace it.*

- *Notice spontaneous thoughts and feelings.*

- *Sit in this space until the experience feels complete. Your imagination easily reveals what you have learned.*

UNSTICK & UP-WICK

Your Intense Emotion + An Event = Stuck Memories

What you feel is what you get, regardless of what you think!
—DEBORAH SANDELLA

Did you ever wake up to find a day that broke up your mind, destroyed your notion of circular time?
—JAGGER/RICHARD LYRICS "SWAY" FROM STICKY FINGERS

When you unstick sabotaging feelings and wick up self-affirming ones, you get an extraordinary boost in physical vitality, clarity, and personal power. Richard, Rachel, and Jennifer's stories illustrate how it works, which is quicker than you think.

RICHARD'S STORY: UNEXPECTED TRIGGERS CAN UNEARTH BURIED FEELINGS

Richard is an amazing entrepreneur. His many successful businesses are flourishing, and he's still looking for more. It's the creative process he loves—getting a vision and watching it materialize like magic.

At a business seminar, Richard volunteers to help demonstrate how we have choices even when we think we don't. The trainer invites Richard to join him onstage and asks him to identify a time when he didn't have a choice. Richard replies, "When I paid my taxes." The facilitator then asks Richard if there is someone whom he loves dearly; the answer is his eleven-year-old daughter Peggy.

Acting out an imaginary scene, the presenter pretends to hold a gun to Peggy's head and says she'll be killed if Richard pays his taxes. It's obvious to everyone including Richard that he would choose not to pay his taxes if it meant his daughter's life. He would risk jail or worse to keep his daughter alive. And so the point is made: we always have a choice.

After Richard leaves the stage, he grows increasingly agitated. Pacing the hall outside the meeting room, he can't forget the image of his daughter with a gun to her head; this image makes him so mad he threatens to "punch out the presenter." No matter how hard he tries, the image won't go away. Knowing from experience that what he imagines frequently manifests, he's terrified that he's causing harm to his daughter.

Richard is a "man's man" who doesn't believe in psychology. He acknowledges he would never go to psychotherapy; however, he's in such pain about his daughter's safety, he seeks immediate assistance at the conference. As Richard's eyes close, he focuses on what's calling for attention in his body. He notices a knot in his stomach where there's extreme tension. Focusing on this tangible knot, he moves into its tightest spot and allows the physical pain as much as possible. As he rests in it, the pain eases, and with a suggestion, he senses an image of the person to whom he needs to speak. His imagination instantly produces the image of his dad and his three daughters. As he senses his family, he tries to hold back the tears, but breaks into sobs of sadness. With this release the pressure decreases, and he identifies the specific image; it's his dad who had passed away six years ago, prior to Richard's divorce. With encouragement, Richard speaks aloud what he's feeling:

I miss you so much, Dad. You were always there for me and now you are gone. I feel so guilty I couldn't make my marriage work. I know you would have wanted us to be a family. I feel I've disappointed you terribly.

Richard finds the energy of the "disappointed" feeling in his body and speaks from it:

I should have been able to make it work, but I just couldn't. I've been very good about providing for everyone. They're taken care of. Dad, can you ever forgive me?

Moving his awareness into his dad, Richard senses what his father wants to say:

Richard, I love you and trust you. I always have and I always will, even in my death. Of course, it was sad when you divorced, but I don't blame you. I knew you were doing what was best. I saw the difficulties between you and Helen, and I understood. Please forgive yourself, Richard; it's time to let go. I'm always with you and the kids. It's okay.

Receiving Dad's love like a stream of colored energy into his body, Richard allows the flow of brilliant white light into his heart until it's filled. Thanking Dad and sensing his loving presence, Richard turns toward his three daughters. Peggy draws his attention first. She's the daughter for whom he was frightened onstage. She's the youngest and most vulnerable. He fears she's been damaged by the divorce, and voices his feelings, which have been unspoken till now:

> Peggy, I love you so much. I'm so sorry it didn't work out with your mother. I wanted to make it work, I just couldn't. Now I'm worried about you because we used to see more of each other, but now not so much. I don't want you to feel abandoned, because you aren't—it was the marriage I left, not you or your siblings. I would do anything for you. What can I do to show you?

Richard moves his awareness into Peggy to sense her response:

> Daddy, I know you love me. I may be young, but I'm smart. I saw how you and Mom were fighting. It wasn't good. I have my sister and brother and that really helps. With the three of us together, I'm not alone. And yes, I would like to see more of you. Maybe we could have a regular time each week when just the two of us go out for fun. I would like that, and I'd feel special.

Richard agrees it would be good to have regular time together and vows to arrange it when he gets home from the seminar.

As Richard turns his attention to his other two daughters, it's clear they don't need him like Peggy. They are more involved with their peers and creating independent lives. They feel loved.

Looking inside his body, Richard now registers very different feelings. The terror and fear are completely gone, and he feels light. He's at peace with his life for the first time since his decision to divorce. This stage event has acted as a tipping point to allow his underlying guilt and sadness to surface. Now that he visibly sees the issues, however, he can dissolve them and take action to improve his relationship with Peggy. Richard's story demonstrates how seemingly unrelated events can coalesce to stimulate healing, if they are allowed to.

RACHAEL'S STORY: WHAT WE FEEL IS STRONGER THAN WHAT WE THINK

It's mid-afternoon and Rachael is in her office working away, which is her habit. The phone rings. It's a hospital in Texas where her oldest daughter Rose lives. The nurse tells her: "Your daughter is in critical condition with liver failure. We're concerned she won't make it. You better call the family and come down right away." Rachael immediately hops a flight and, committed to do whatever it takes to keep Rose alive, begins researching liver transplants. She discovers getting Rose on a transplant waiting list is more difficult than she thought. Still, Rachael is a strong woman who has achieved amazing results in the past and she's determined to beat the odds.

After a week of working tirelessly to infuse her daughter with hope and engage the medical resources to extend her life, Rachael walks into the hospital room and gasps in horror. She sees a face that's extremely bloated and scary green. The whites of Rose's eyes are solid red. Her liver has failed; her time has run out. Saving her isn't going to happen.

Losing a child is the greatest pain a parent can face, and Rachael dips into serious grieving. Being a very positive woman, she works hard to look through optimistic eyes. "*My baby is finally free of pain*," Rachael tells herself as many of us do when our love ones die. Also, she connects with her daughter's presence during meditation, which feels reassuring.

During the following two years, Rachael has several serious illnesses and injuries that bring her close to death. At a gut level, she knows her life depends on doing something different, but she has no idea what. She's worked with the pain of her daughter's death in every way she knows, yet it's still present.

About this time, Rachael gets a notice about an event with a noted psychic who communicates with those who have passed over, and she decides to attend. The hotel ballroom is filled with an audience of middle-aged men and women. Rachael hopes this is her chance to heal; after all, the timing of the event is perfect. Instead she faces another disappointment—she's not chosen from the audience to receive a reading, and the depth of her sadness hits bottom.

The next day, Rachael's in excruciating pain. During her regular meditation, the RIM process she learned years earlier surfaces in her mind, and she immediately senses the sadness in her body. It feels gooey, dark, and especially suffocating. Though extremely uncomfortable, she bravely embraces the yucky energy as much as she can, and an image of her daughter appears. Expecting to see the daughter she loves, she involuntarily gasps in terror as it is the ghastly, green face that presents itself. This scary face isn't her sweet daughter and she tries to make the nightmarish image go away, but it's stuck. Being a highly spiritual person, Rachael tries to connect with her daughter's evolved spirit, but the monster face remains.

Realizing she can't control it, Rachael finally addresses the image honestly:

You aren't my daughter; she was sweet and loving. You are scary and dead. I don't want to remember you this way. It's too hard. It makes me feel so guilty I didn't do more to keep you alive. You did so well for such a long time, but this last year, you deteriorated and it was so hard to see. I wanted to support you in rising above the issues, but it didn't work and I don't know if I can ever forgive myself. It's just too painful to bear. I would do anything to get you back, even kill myself. Even as I speak it, I know this won't help your soul or mine.

Rachael sobs until there's a release. She notices the green face has faded and been replaced by a smiling, normal-looking image of her daughter Rose. She continues:

I'm sorry, Honey. I love you so much. I always have and I always will. I wish I had done something different, but I also realize you had your own journey regardless of what I did. I now am willing to respect your journey—your decision—although I miss you terribly. Yes, I love connecting in spirit, but I'm sad to not have you physically sitting next to me. I haven't wanted to admit that because it made it real, but I feel it regardless of what I say. I can't talk myself out of it anymore. If I could, it would have worked because I've tried really hard. I also notice, as I'm expressing these feelings honestly, I feel a release and a lightness I haven't felt since your passing.

Rachael finally feels greater peace. She may always miss her daughter, but she now feels a sense of completion. Her life-threatening illnesses/injuries disappear, and a year later she meets someone with whom she falls in love. A new chapter of her life begins.

Her story shows us how feelings are stronger than intellectual rationalizations. What you feel is more powerful than what you think. Yet, when feelings are allowed, they quickly flow toward a natural course of recovery.

JENNIFER'S STORY: MAKING FRIENDS WITH OUR FEARS

Jennifer loves being pregnant. She feels great with each pregnancy and gives birth to two healthy, beautiful boys. It's hard to imagine that her 5′ 2″ body can carry an extra fifty pounds each time, but it does. However, the pressure has resulted in stress incontinence. She jokes, "I can't walk and laugh at the same time without peeing." She feels she's too young to wear adult diapers, so corrective surgery it is.

At the time, her condition has resulted in some more serious issues, and surgery is an inpatient process. Jennifer is hospitalized for two days; to prepare, she requests a RIM process to calm her nerves. With eyes closed she senses the anxieties in her body and greets them one by one. Most are related to butterflies in her stomach. As she eventually moves her attention into the butterflies, they spontaneously fly out of her body and into the room, which happens to look like a cold, barren operating room.

Seeing this imagined room where she will undergo surgery makes her shiver; it looks harsh and stark. She notices the sharp instruments on a table beside a bare bed, and her anxiety increases. She feels fearful thinking of her unconscious body in this room with intrusive things being done to her without her awareness. The sharp instruments make her the most nervous and remind her that she will be cut.

When asked to speak aloud to the instruments, with closed eyes she begins:

I'm not sure about you. You scare me. Thinking about you cutting into my body just isn't good. I asked for this surgery, but you feel so cold and barren. You are going to cut me without knowing who I am or caring about who I am. I don't matter to you and that doesn't feel good.

As Jennifer senses the scalpel receiving all she's expressed like a stream of colored energy, something quite magical happens—the instruments come alive like the cups and saucers in the movie *Beauty and the Beast* and begin to dance in the air and sing the movie song "Be My Guest." Jennifer spontaneously begins to laugh and her whole presence shifts from suspiciousness to playfulness:

> Everything in the operating room is coming alive like a delight-ful cartoon singing and dancing around me. It's quite fun. I'm dancing with them now and the room doesn't look bare or scary anymore. It's full of sparkles and light and I feel really good here. Everything here is my friend and likes me.

She chuckles, realizing her comment probably sounds ridicu-lous, but it's what she's feeling. Jennifer sees this imaginary scene wrap itself around her body like a positive energy blanket, and she easily remembers it.

On her way to the hospital, Jennifer phones to say: "I'm as high as a kite. I can't believe it, I feel so happy, light, and safe. I know everything is going to be fine." And like a fairy tale, it is. Days after her discharge, Jennifer reports she's still feeling high like she's had a special experience, and continues to enjoy the delight of it.

Jennifer's experience demonstrates the natural flow of healing that comes from making friends with one's fears. Furthermore, we see how intense positive feelings like delight, love, peace, joy, etc., also create a biochemical event that automatically anchors in body memory.

HOW IT WORKS—PRACTICALLY AND SCIENTIFICALLY

What do feelings and glue have in common? As we con-tinue to look at emotion through a physical filter, we find that adhesives offer a metaphor for understanding how cer-tain memories get stuck in the mind/body while others do not. Adhesives activate a chemical reaction with an external energy source. For example, in 1839, Charles Goodyear dis-covered adhesives could be made by heating rubber with sul-fur. With the invention of the automobile, stronger and more durable adhesives were needed, and rubber was treated with strong acids to create rubber cement for bonding metal to rubber. The greater the intensity of the chemical reaction, the stronger the adhesion.

Similarly, the greater the emotional intensity of an event, the more strongly the feelings get stuck in the nervous system. Strong feelings create a biochemical change, and when highly charged (negatively or positively), they gain immense stickiness in the body. In contrast, neutral experiences are easily forgotten.

For example, Richard was a very savvy businessperson, but he felt uncontrollable panic after playing out the imaginary scene of his daughter's life being threatened. He knew intellectually it wasn't real, yet his underground guilt was leaking out in a big, indirect way.

Similarly, Rachael thought she'd grieved for her daughter's death; however, her guilt and despair were stuck. Her horrific last memory was completely unexpected, and the brain remembers surprising events more vividly. Her conscious resistance to this ugly image was inhibiting her grieving. Subsequent self-destructive experiences were the visible sign that ugly feelings were stuck beneath the surface.

The good news is that both Richard and Rachael were able to reveal the adhered emotions and *unstick* them immediately. We all have this ability; we just haven't understood how our emotional operating system works—until now. Are you ready?

As you've read in several of the real-life stories shared, intensely painful feelings and images elicit inner experiences like being trapped, suffocated, and stuck in tar. The longer an issue has been underground, the stickier it grows. It takes on a life of its own that is outside the influence of the logical mind, which makes us feel out-of-control and anxious.

In their book *Buddha's Brain*, authors Rick Hanson and Richard Mendius demonstrate how the reptilian part of our brains is predisposed to avoiding harm over seeking gain.[1] When our cave-dwelling ancestors were at risk of encountering a saber-toothed tiger, it was paramount to be alert to potential danger. Surviving depended upon avoiding danger more than enjoying life. Thus, we're quicker to have a highly charged reaction to negative experiences than to positive ones. Positive experiences must significantly outnumber the scary ones for us to feel safe.

Psychiatrist Bessel Van Der Kolk in his book *The Body Keeps the Score* points out how our instinctual urges for safety must be addressed for relief. He explains that though psychology has usually tried to help people gain insight and understanding to manage their behavior:

> Neuroscience research shows that very few psychological problems are defects in understanding; most originate in pressures from deeper regions in the brain that drive our perception and attention. When the alarm bell of the emotional brain [ancient brain and limbic system] keeps signaling that you are in danger, no amount of insight will silence it.[2]

This hypervigilance in our brain sometimes shows up directly during a RIM process. For many years, Paige was plagued with an ache between her left ear and eye that just wouldn't go away. She'd been tested by numerous and varied doctors and dentists with no clear findings.

Closing her eyes, she moves through her body, following a series of sensations in her head, gut, and heart. This self-generated process slowly eases her into a deep inner body awareness that uncovers a primal experience. She spontaneously feels the sensation of lying on the cold ground in a dark cave. Her body is unable to relax because she must stay tuned to potential danger. She hears the sound of a twig breaking along with heavy breathing, and her body freezes in absolute terror. Being a woman with children, she feels completely helpless and incapable of fighting off a predator. She is paralyzed in an intense and immediate feeling of threat to her survival!

Asking her imagination to give form to the terror in her body, Paige senses massive blackness in her gut; it's a bottomless void and she shudders to sense it inside her. With encouragement, she bravely and gradually moves her attention into it as her fear intensifies. As she stays in the scary blackness, she doesn't die, and the dark energy gradually lightens until she begins feeling calm. Over time, four distinct experiences of identifying and embracing inner survival terrors dissolve the ear pain she has suffered for so long.

Paige survived a "crazy" childhood. Having grown up with alcoholic parents, she is still stuck in feeling like a helpless child who's afraid for herself and her younger brother. In reality, she's married with children; however, the stickiness of primal fear is stronger than reality. For forty-four years, she's been executing her daily activities as if her life depends on doing things perfectly. Intellectually, she understands her faulty thinking, but her gut is stuck in the fear of annihilation. After dissolving the primal fear, she understands that she isn't crazy after all. Rather, she's unraveled the fearful feeling. Furthermore, she's acquired new body memories of dissolving energy blocks by embracing them and receiving a newly felt calm. She's learning how to create her own safety.

Our issues may seem obvious, but an illogical rush of emotion can cloud everything. I wrote the following whimsical fable inspired by *The Princess and the Pea* fairy tale by Hans Christian Andersen to illustrate the simplicity of how it works.

....

The Prince and the Stone

Once upon a time, there lived a Prince in a faraway land. He grew up in a huge castle with many brothers and sisters. As the oldest, he was considered the ranking royalty amongst the brood, which caused him to be the object of many pranks by the others. His twin brothers Hit and Miss were especially aggravating. They constantly played tricks, and his emotional reaction gratified them more than sweets. The Prince might be the highest-ranking sibling, but as quick as a wink, they could play havoc with his majesty.

One night, the twins decide to hide a jagged stone under the Prince's mattress and interrupt his rest—and it works. The next day the Prince is frantic with fatigue for not sleeping. He is practicing for athletic competitions, and as the royal, he fervently wants to win. He decides to stack an extra mattress on his bed, hoping to induce sleep with greater softness and comfort. However, he sleeps not. Again and again, day after day he adds more mattresses to improve his rest until stacks of layers are piled high to the ceiling. Yet, he still is restless and unsettled. In fact, he is growing more restless with the failure of each new layer.

Things are seriously wrong now, as the Prince cannot ignore the problem and is at his wit's end—literally he is so tired he is unable to think and the big competition is the next day. As he climbs to his perch atop the many mattresses, which requires a tall ladder and considerably more energy, he becomes aware of how much effort it's costing him to maintain these layers. The mattresses have done nothing to improve his comfort, so he might as well remove them and return his bed to its simplicity. He has nothing to lose—he's not sleeping anyway. At least he'll feel like himself again.

And so the Prince spends half the night ridding his bed of the extra mattresses. One by one he maneuvers each layer in a unique way so it will fall safely. Then he shifts them to the extra chamber beside his room where his footman will remove them the following day. It takes some muscle, but finally his room feels like his own again, which is a nice feeling.

Having released any expectation of sleep, he lies in his bed with its rightful mattress. Without all those extra layers, his body focuses on something that isn't right. With his attention on his body, he feels there is one spot definitely out of whack.

Lifting the mattress to inspect the underside, he spies it—the troublesome stone, which he immediately knows was placed by the mischievous twins. Ah . . . he is surprised by how good it feels to discover what has been disturbing his sleep. Now it all makes sense, and he relaxes more than he has since the beginning of all this restlessness.

He quickly falls asleep with a smile on his face, dreams sweet dreams, and excels in the competition the next day.

The Prince and the Stone offers a metaphor for how easy it is to build layers of protection in an effort to avoid discomfort. We do this all the time. Sometimes the original event is minor, and we add a thin layer. Other times, the issue is unbearable and has built up over time. Accommodating the weight is burdensome and significantly interrupts normal life. The good news/bad news of it is that the layers create distance between us and the perceived danger, and the distance creates an illusion of greater safety. The same distance, however, prevents us from confronting and resolving the root problem, so we suffer indefinitely.

When we bravely dive into our layers, we shift from a fear-based state and activate our inner self-healing system. Once you know what's really happening inside you, you can mobilize your innate resources and use them to solve the problem quickly.

Ask your imagination for a number for how many "stones" are disrupting your peace. As you sense this number, move your attention into your heart where you hear a word or words that identify these stones. Write them down, so you can work with them in the Practice It Yourself section. Take a minute . . .

Whose Feelings Are You Having?

When the Boston Marathon bombing occurred in April 2013, my daughter was a senior at Boston University and living near the neighborhood where the shooter was loose. She and I were glued to the television and frequently on the phone during the citywide lockdown.

There were hundreds of witnesses at the immediate scene of the explosion. Some of the victims were dead, and others were missing limbs. Journalists on the scene reported: "I can't get these images out of my head." Following the bombing, a study published in the journal *Proceedings of the National Academy of Sciences* found: "Acute stress symptoms increased with each additional hour of bombing-related media exposure via television, social media, videos, print, or radio." The U.S. Department of Veteran Affairs Center for PTSD concludes there is a link between watching news of traumatic events, such as terrorist attacks, and stress symptoms. They also found that people who have experienced previous trauma suffer a cumulative effect with intensified reactions. A University of California, Irvine study challenges the key assumption that direct exposure is necessary to develop stress-related problems.[3] In other words, seeing intense and scary images creates a biochemical event that's sticky whether we are experiencing them directly or through empathy with others. The bombing has taught us that images of another's pain can get stuck in our awareness.

Empathy has been traced to the presence of *mirror neurons* in the brain. Initially, an Italian researcher noticed a monkey's brain was firing (registering on the computer screen) as if picking up a peanut or a banana when, in fact, the monkey was watching the researcher do these actions.[4] These mirror neurons explain empathy and imitation. It's worthwhile to keep track of how much exposure to media stories of trauma you can manage before it sends you over the edge. Notice when you need to turn the radio and television off and do something soothing.

With the breaking news of 9/11, I immediately had a strong sense I could not watch the constant television coverage. Instead, I held the intention of healing for the victims and their families while walking or meditating. During the Boston Marathon bombing, I was less effective at maintaining emotional autonomy because of the connection with my daughter. It was interesting to note the difference.

It's important to discern which feelings are real and which are empathic so you can manage the stress effectively. Allowing yourself to become empathic to the point of being traumatized by another's experience is unnecessary and ineffective.

Connie was a first responder to the 2012 Aurora Century 16 theater shooting in Colorado, when a madman burst into a midnight premiere of the new Batman movie, jumped onstage, and began randomly shooting automatic weapons into the audience. Twelve people were killed and seventy injured. Shortly after the incident, Connie gains weight and increased glaucoma eye pressure. When she calls to accept a pro bono RIM Institute offer for those suffering from this crisis, she mentions she's been meditating regularly, exercising more, and eating less, yet her weight and eye pressure continue to be elevated since the shooting. In other words, something is stuck.

When Connie begins her phone session, she focuses on her breathing and follows it in and out until she is in a relaxed, meditative state. Scanning her body, she finds a tightness in her eyes, especially the left one. As she gives it her attention, her imagination manifests the form of a yellow square behind her eyes. The square is solid and heavy with sharp edges. It's the sharpness that draws her attention most, so she moves into the sharpest part and asks for an image of the source of this sharpness.

Connie instantly senses a scene of attending the survivors of the theater killings. Her assignment is simple: she is encouraging family and friends of victims onto buses to transport them to crisis services for immediate counseling. The image before her is specific: it's the moment she runs into a couple she knows. She says hello to them, and they share that they are the grandparents of someone who has died. They engage with Connie about the unbelievable murder of their precious granddaughter, and Connie is emotionally dying because she can't even imagine the unbearable pain of losing her own grandson Josh. Her empathy for them is off the charts.

During her session, Connie regains her emotional autonomy through an imaginary talk with these grandparents:

I'm so sorry. I don't know what to say. I'm immobilized with guilt that I have my grandson while you have lost your precious granddaughter. It feels so bad to even consider the possibility of losing Josh. Even as I speak of it, I realize I'm struggling to handle something I don't have to face. I feel great compassion for you and I wish there were something I could say or do that would help, yet I realize there's nothing that can take away your pain. As these things are spoken, I feel better. I do not have to grieve for my grandson. He is still here with me, for which I feel great gratitude. I feel great compassion for your loss, and I hope you find solace. I will hold you in my prayers.

Connie still feels compassion, but no longer is personalizing the couple's experience as her own. This important reality check takes nothing away from them. Rather, when Connie is clear about her emotional boundaries, she can be more available to them because she's not fighting off her own reaction; it gets to be about them.

When Compassion Works Better than Empathy

Empathy is understanding how another feels by standing in that person's shoes and feeling the same feelings. The mirror neurons mentioned earlier automatically make us aware of another's emotions and unconsciously reproduce them. This is one of the ways we are neurologically wired to be in relationships. People inherently display various degrees of empathy.

The word *empathy* originated in the early 1900s and derives from the Greek word *empátheia,* meaning "affection," and is equivalent to *em (emphasis)* + path- (base of *páschein-,* "to suffer"). Thus, it means "to suffer out of affection."[5] It is a consistent aspect of health care provider training to maintain an environment of caring within the boundaries of a professional relationship. More recently, it has been identified as an essential ingredient for successful couples' and parenting communication. As a mother, I have found empathy to be the best way to read the mind of a crying baby who isn't able to say what's wrong.

Too little or too much empathy can get you into trouble. For example, people who are focused on themselves to the exclusion of others' feelings are considered narcissistic, while those who overidentify with others' emotions frequently lose touch with their own sense of self. Balancing on the empathetic continuum means returning to the center point between uncaring detachment and submersion in another's pain. Error on the uncaring side prevents intimate, loving relationships, while error on the overcaring end interrupts healthy self-care. We see in Connie's story how her health deteriorated when she overidentified with another's loss.

Furthermore, when we feel another's emotion, it energetically releases their pressure to take action. For example, it's common for the wives of unhealthy men to worry. Although that's understandable, it may energetically lessen their husband's sense of responsibility, which may result in less behavioral change.

In other words, the wife who is overly empathic may feel the intensity and necessity for a change more than her husband, but doesn't have control over his behavior. The husband may feel taken care of and a lessened burden to change.

When my husband was about to turn fifty, he wanted to be in charge of his midlife crisis, so we planned a family sabbatical to Australia. During that year, I was on holiday and not working for the first time since the sixth grade. Being out of the fishbowl of ordinary life, I realized I was more in touch with my clients' feelings than my own. It was a big shock for a psychotherapist! On the other hand, this realization allowed me to use that year as a profound time of getting to know myself again. After our return to the States, I made self-awareness a priority, which naturally allowed me to have better boundaries. Interestingly, my previous symptoms of allergies and fatigue disappeared, and the people around me became more responsible for themselves.[6]

As I have developed and taught the RIM technique over the last twenty years, I've been more attentive to preventing the professional burnout sometimes called caregiver fatigue. I've observed some people are naturally empathic, while others need to learn to become more empathic. It's been effective to help students identify where they are on the empathy continuum and work to stay in balance.

Furthermore, I've learned to encourage compassion rather than empathy when engaging with others who are traumatized. Feeling others' pain is not only unnecessary, it can get in the way.

The prefix *com-* in compassion means "with," "together," "in association," and "with intensive force." The definition of *passion* is "any powerful or compelling emotion or feeling, as love or hate."[7] We can walk compassionately with others and appreciate their intense emotions without taking on their feeling or suffering.

In a different vein, empathic awareness of how others view us is essential to good relationships. When we see ourselves through another's eyes, we gain valuable insight and direction. You've seen this process in action in the real-life stories. When clients have imaginary dialogues with another, they move their attention into that person and look from those eyes to sense what wants to be spoken and to voice it for them. Frequently, speaking empathically for another in this imaginary way can naturally resolve relationship issues without an actual conversation. Recently, a husband and wife engaged in individual RIM processes. It was amazing to see how it improved their intimacy even without having a couples' session. Both uprooted deep childhood anger, which caused their frustration with each other to evaporate. Rather, a sense of affection for their partnership increased. The wife explained that instead of anger, compassion for her husband now pops into her mind whenever he is acting childish because she compassionately remembers sensing his original childhood wound. You'll learn more about this kind of empathy in chapter six.

To discern a clear sense of emotional boundaries with empathic awareness, the client doesn't imagine *being* this person; rather they *sense* what's happening inside this character and speak it for them. This compassionate, imaginary speaking allows life-changing insights without losing one's autonomy.

How Empathic Are You?

Ask your imagination for a number from one to ten for how empathic you are, with ten being most. Receive whatever number pops into your mind first and circle it below.

1	2	3	4	5	6	7	8	9	10

Next ask your imagination for a number from one to ten of what is the optimum level of empathy for a healthy you and circle it below.

| 1 | 2 | 3 | 4 | 5 | 6 | 7 | 8 | 9 | 10 |

Move your attention into the *optimum empathy* number and sense how it feels as you look over at an image of you when out of balance. You'll naturally see the differences between where you have been and what would be healthier.

Unsticking Negative Emotion

Keep Breathing

The first and immediate thing to do when you find yourself stuck in terror is to breathe! We know from wild animal research that the reptilian brain automatically assumes annihilation and forgets everything except survival. Such emotions can send us into the panic mode of fight, flight, freeze, or faint (even when the danger is imagined), so we react without regard to reality. We automatically collapse into a mindless/bodiless state of panic to eliminate the threat. We saw this response in Richard's story, when, completely out of character, he wanted to punch the presenter who had suggested the scary image of his daughter.

The visceral response to danger may express itself in emotional or physical distancing, loss of consciousness, or an offensive attack on the source of the danger to scare it away. The feeling may be high anxiety, numbness, or rage, depending on our patterns. When we're afraid, we tend to hold our breath, which keeps us physically stuck in this primitive fear.

Because breath connects the voluntary and involuntary nervous systems as mentioned in chapter two, it offers a natural bridge from mindless panic to mindful awareness of body sensation and thought. We shift from submersion in animalistic response to conscious awareness of being a thinking/feeling human being. Concentrating on your breathing gradually returns you to awareness of yourself and your ability to think.[8]

Being guided in detailed and unfamiliar ways of breathing successfully engages the rational mind, which accelerates relaxation. The left brain becomes present when there are instructions unfamiliar enough to capture its attention and simple enough to be easily done. You now have the emotional and rational parts of the brain working together to solve the problem.

Myra, a manager who has been on stress leave from her executive position at an insurance company, closes her eyes. As she gives her attention to her breathing, she naturally relaxes; however, when it's suggested she imagine inhaling through her eyes and exhaling through her navel, she is keenly attentive. Her overactive perfectionism is now engaged inward—a big switch. Neurologically, her body is shifting out of its habit of straining to overachieve in the world and focuses inward. Wow! What a boost to focus on one's inner experience with intensity. Afterward, she says: "Breathing through my eyes—that really got me. I've never felt so relaxed. My whole body feels healthier. My stomachache and restlessness are gone." You can play with a number of unusual breathing activities in the Practice It Yourself section at the end of this chapter.

See and Hear Yourself

When our eyes are open, we constantly scan the environment. It is a habit retained from our cave dweller days. In fact, when researcher Timothy Wilson at the University of Virginia gave people fifteen minutes to let their minds wander—"to sit and do nothing but think"—people were so desperate for distraction, they chose mild electric shock over being alone with themselves. Six of the twenty-four women shocked themselves, while twelve of the eighteen men did so. Most people shocked themselves around seven times during the fifteen minutes.[9] Wilson suggests we are so accustomed to being distracted by smartphones, computers, television, coworkers, and family members, we've grown unfamiliar with being with ourselves.

When you close your eyes and sense your inner sensations, however, attention shifts. You become the subject of your attention, and you are free to follow spontaneous inner sensations as discussed as "mind wandering" in chapter two. With your attention in your body, there's a myriad of possibilities you may notice—discomfort in your right shoulder, heaviness in your left thigh, spinning in your head. Because it's all personal to you, you can't do it wrong. How often does that happen?

Your body loves to have your attention, the way children love to be the apple of their parents' eye. When you connect with your body in this way, you create an intimate relationship with yourself—an inner experience of being seen and heard. Who doesn't want that? Still, we tend to look for it from others. Now you are learning how to find it within yourself.

Rick demonstrates the immense power of how sensing oneself loosens sticky memories. The minute he closes his eyes, he begins to cry, though there's no specific feeling connected with the tears. As he welcomes them, he relaxes. There is no need to hide anything. In fact, with encouragement he embraces the tears by imagining being inside them, where he finds an unexpected feeling of safety and protection. He senses a deep settling into himself, including the unpleasant parts, and an unfamiliar kind of peace arrives—it feels good.

After a while, Rick's imagination brings him a spontaneous image of himself at five years old standing in the bathtub and crying. Little Rick is feeling lost when adult Rick finds him. His dad, a military man, is very demanding, and little Rick feels unable to do anything right. He's lonely all the time because there's no one to turn to for guidance and support. Little Rick is extremely confused that the person who ought to be comforting him is actually the source of intense discomfort. He feels alone, unloved, and helpless.

As adult Rick watches his younger self, there comes an awareness of their differences. The grown-up man has developed many resources not available to the little boy. Adult Rick has attracted a wise and loving fatherlike friend who has supported him and diminished his feeling alone. He's become very successful with a loving family, successful business, and a respected place in his community.

The father-figure friend gets called forth for virtual support, and Rick feels his supportive hand on his right shoulder. The support becomes multilayered: virtual friend with adult Rick and adult Rick with little Rick. Adult Rick embraces the helpless child and comforts him. The knowing adult soothes the childish fears and reassures him that he's capable and competent and going to have a great life when he grows up. The adult finishes with: "I love you, little Rick."

As the emotional dust settles, the adult shifts attention to being little Rick to fully receive the adult's love. Looking out from little Rick's eyes, his imagination colors the energy bright blue as it flows from the adult into his little boy body. They both are graphically lighting up with intense blue love that fills them and spills into the whole room. Child and adult visually and emotionally receive comfort and reassurance.

As Rick turns attention to the inside of little Rick's body, the blue energy is pervasive, but he finds a black, sludge-like pain in the throat area. When asked what he wants to do, little Rick says: "Get rid of it." The father-figure friend, when asked for help, imagines an emotional vacuum cleaner that sucks out the black energy and recycles it into fertile soil.[10] As the black energy disappears, the blue energy spreads into the little boy's throat, while having someone to help him instills feelings of worthiness.

Adult Rick returns to his adult self, looks over at the four-year-old, and spontaneously chuckles: "Oh, my little Rick! You look so different with bright, smiling eyes." The little boy projects a feeling of knowing who he is and where he is going. Rick experiences loving himself in a deep, visceral way because he is seen and heard by himself. Well-known author Brené Brown has shared how "being seen" as your authentically vulnerable self rather than trying to be perfect is key in developing a feeling of worthiness to be loved. She calls this "wholehearted" living.[11] When you consistently see and hear yourself, you develop a confidence that is unshakable. You aren't dependent on others for reassurance, rather you can actually feel security in your own body.

Ask your imagination for a number from one to ten as to how much you are seeing and hearing yourself, with ten being the most.

| 1 | 2 | 3 | 4 | 5 | 6 | 7 | 8 | 9 | 10 |

If you aren't at ten, jump into the ten level and notice what that feels like in comparison. You will get to play with this in the Practice It Yourself section.

Wicking Up Juicy Good Feelings

Interestingly, the same process for *unsticking undesirable emotion* effectively *wicks up desirable emotions*. The physics of emotion demonstrates that moving toward and allowing your feelings activate your emotional operating system, which naturally discerns between negative and positive feelings and responds appropriately. When we move toward and allow all feelings, our system organically dissolves the dammed ones and expands the affirming ones. Your feelings are smarter than you think!

Asking for an Image That Represents an Answer or Issue

As you've seen in other chapters, your imagination can pull random thoughts, memories, and ideas from thin air to address your questions in amazing ways. My friend Jack Canfield has shared a great example.

He and coauthor Mark Victor Hansen had decided to write a book of 101 inspiring human stories that consistently brought tears and laughter to their audiences. When they were looking for a title, Jack decided to meditate on it. As he slipped into a deeper state of relaxation, he lost sight of the specific question and experienced a floating feeling common in meditation. Out of the blue, he sensed a hand spontaneously writing on an imaginary blackboard. What did it write? *Chicken Soup for the Soul.* He realized this was the title he'd requested, and a shiver moved through his body. The first *Chicken Soup for the Soul* book became a *New York Times* best seller and turned into a series of books and multimillion-dollar sales.

Sticky problems can be solved in the same way. Ruth's imagination brought her a very interesting answer to her issue. She is in a new relationship after her divorce. Although she likes this new man, they are running into some conflicts. When Ruth closes her eyes and asks her imagination for a helpful image representing this conflict, right before her pops up an image of her boyfriend trying to stand on a TV table. She immediately begins to laugh and says: "Oh my, I'm wanting him to do what's impossible, like an adult man standing on a TV table. Now I get what he's been saying. I guess I've been a little overzealous about having this new relationship be on my terms." When she asks her imagination for an image of a healthier relationship, she is given a picture of the two of them dancing—full-size. In tune with each other's movements, they glide together gracefully as one.

Two weeks later, her boyfriend says: "What happened, Ruth? You are completely different." Her relationship is transformed by her new awareness. She now has compassion for him and communicates her needs in more playful and connecting ways. Whenever she remembers that image, she can't help but laugh.

Your imagination is primed to share helpful insights and solutions. You can Practice It Yourself at the end of the chapter.

Integrating New Positive Feelings into Your Body

Once you have new positive feelings, you can help them stick in body memory. Ruth has anchored her new dancing image with her boyfriend (who is now her fiancé) by first sensing all the details and then imagining being herself in the image instead of watching it. Looking out of her new eyes, Ruth viscerally feels the romance and satisfaction of moving together as one. She rests in it until it feels complete—a new experience is anchored in the body.

You can integrate any desirable feeling more deeply. First, you imagine living the experience rather than watching it, until it feels real. Next, sense one word of how it feels and find the specific location of this positive feeling in your body, its color, and its texture. Moving into this good energy and fully sensing it, you create new neurological imprints that light up the brain. For example, Rick, while looking out of the eyes of his four-year-old self, felt love and support from adult Rick. He sensed that this new happiness and confidence looked like a bright blue brilliance with flashes of white light radiating throughout his young body. When Rick moved his attention into it and imagined becoming it, he felt deep confidence and peace at a visceral level. He rested in it until the experience felt complete.

Whenever you enjoy a happy experience, regardless of the reason, you can boost its sticking power in the same way: 1) imagine living the experience; 2) sense the one word of how you are feeling; 3) sense the energy of this feeling in your body, noticing its location, size, shape, color, texture, etc.; and 4) immerse yourself in it.

Similarly, you can rehearse positive images for successful future events like finding the perfect job, giving a presentation, meeting a new partner—it can be any goal. Merely ask your imagination to show you a beneficial video of it. When your thinker isn't the doer, your creative right brain is more engaged. Being in a relaxed state with your eyes closed (maybe soft music, too), you can sense this movie created by your imagination. Some people feel, sense, or hear it more than they actually see it. Imagery is evocative and multisensory; thus, you don't have to see pictures. You can trust the sensory experience will flow through your dominant learning channel. RIM facilitator Dr. Audrey Boxwell finds practicing twice a week for four weeks significantly enhances the benefits of imagery.[12]

PRACTICE IT YOURSELF

Whole Brain Breathing Activities

The following exercises can be used individually or in combination with each other. Although they can be done with your eyes open, the visual channel is distracting, and you'll get better results with your eyes closed (except for kids, who do it easily with wide-open eyes). There are three ways to practice with closed eyes: 1) read each instruction and practice it with your eyes closed before opening your eyes to move on to the next step (some people prefer to read a section, sense their inner experience, and write it down before moving to the next step); 2) make a recording of the script (smartphones work great) and listen to it with your eyes closed; or 3) practice with a partner where the two of you take turns guiding each other.

- Closing your eyes and resting in a comfortable and private place, take a deep cleansing breath in through your nose and exhale through your mouth as you sense your shoulders sinking toward the earth.

- Easily imagine the next breath coming in through your forehead, flowing through your torso, and exiting out your belly button.

- Breathing in through your throat, exhale out of the soles of your feet.

- As you allow an inbreath through your shoulders, it moves through both arms and out the palms of your hands.

- Sensing air flowing in through the front of your body, allow your awareness to follow as it moves through every cell, atom, and molecule and then out of the back of your body. The fresh air and oxygen come in the front and whatever is unnecessary like carbon dioxide and unneeded feelings flow out your back—similar to how exhaust flows from a car. Continue to breathe in this way, till your body feels balanced.

- As your attention rests on your body, notice what area wants more oxygen. As you sense it, notice its size, shape, and color. Moving your attention into this area, easily sense its energy and allow it. Resting in it, notice how more oxygen is called to it with your attention. Enjoy the process and remain here till it feels complete.

Unsticking Feelings Activity

Loosening sticky emotion is like unsticking glue. You have to find the stuck spot and gently give it attention so it can come apart.

- Closing your eyes, focus on breathing and relaxing into the surface upon which you rest as if it were made specifically for you. Take a minute.

- With your attention on the inside of your body, focus on what calls to you first. Notice the size, shape, and color your imagination is giving this area. Does it have a specific shape, or is it amorphous? Is it solid or hollow? Does it have movement or sound? Notice all the details of this energy. (Pause)

- As you sense the quality that is calling you most intensely, move your attention into it as best as you can and rest in it. (Pause)

- As you rest in this energy, your imagination flashes a thought, word, feeling, or image into your mind that represents what's stuck here. You receive the first thing that pops up, letting go of any desire to edit. (Pause)

- Sensing what word, image, or memory has been revealed, you notice the details and feel of it. (Pause)

- Being in the energy of what's here, you notice how its intensity diminishes as you allow it. Take as much time as you need, as you sense it neutralizing. (Pause)

- Take your time to return your attention to the room. As you become aware of your body again, all the valuable insights return with your conscious awareness.

- When you are ready, you take some time to write down your experiences and insights. (Research shows writing about your experience after the imagery boosts the benefits.)

Seeing and Hearing Yourself Activity

- With your eyes closed, your imagination calls forth an image of you as a child.

- You receive the first image that pops up and welcome it.

- Noticing how you look, hold this child in whatever way feels right.

The Adult You Talks to the Little You

- Being with her/him, you sense what needs to be said to this precious, innocent you. Go ahead and speak to your little self in your mind or write it down on paper.

The Little You Receives from the Adult You

- Bring your attention into the little you, look at the adult you, and receive what's been expressed like a stream of colored energy. Notice the color and quality and where it enters your body.

- As you sense this energy filling up your little body, notice how this feels and write it down.

- Exchange a hug if it feels right.

- As your little self, you notice how the adult self looks from this perspective.

The Adult You Acknowledges the Little You

- Moving your attention back into your adult self, look over at your child self. Notice how this child's eyes, face, and body look different now and write it down.

- Let the child know you are always here for him/her, and if both agree, the two of you make plans for the best time and place to connect regularly.

Wicking Up Positive Emotions Activity

We can create emotional superglue to allow self-affirming, positive emotions to stick. In the following activity, call up a specific positive outcome you want to happen. You are going to create a new brain memory of this success happening in the present time. Thus, you create emotional memory, similar to how we create muscle memory by practicing physical activities. Repeat this activity at least twice daily for thirty days.

- Select the positive outcome you want to wick up.

- Put on some relaxing music and focus on your breathing until you are very relaxed. Letting go of needing to do anything, ride your breath as your belly rises and falls. Take some time.

- As you rest in a deeper level of relaxation, your imagination flashes an image of you being successful at this selected situation.

- As you sense this successful you, notice all the details of how you look and how you're dressed—including the color and style of your clothes and shoes.

- Looking into these successful eyes, notice what emotion you sense.

- As you observe this image, you naturally notice how you are talking, moving, and making decisions as confidence radiates from your body, through your eyes, and in your smile. Take a moment to appreciate this image of you as fully as possible.

- As you sense how success looks on you, move your attention into the successful you to look out of these eyes and sense your feet and feel grounded in this successful body all the way down to your toes, out to the tips of your fingers, and up to the top of your head. Rest in this place until it feels complete.

- With your attention focused inward, sense this feeling of success in your own body. Where it is? What is its color and texture? Sense all the details of it you can.

- As you sense this energy of confidence, move into it and immerse yourself—swimming and splashing and laughing and soaking it up. Take as much time as you want. Feeling a sense of completion, you know it's always present even after you open your eyes.

- When you are ready, open your eyes and notice the confident feeling in your body. Focusing attention on this new body feeling, describe it on paper and keep this paper beside your bed or next to the bathroom mirror to read and experience daily.

Your feet nailed to the floor
An imaginary hammer appears and you grab it
Freeing yourself feels strong
You travel inner paradises never before seen
You are stronger than nails

ME & THEE

Your Wholeness Is Greater Than the Sum of Your Human Parts

Indeed, man has always been seeking wholeness—mental, physical, social, and individual. It is instructive to consider the word "health" in English is based on an Anglo-Saxon word "hale" meaning "whole:" that is, to be healthy is to be whole. Likewise the English "holy" is based on the same root as "whole." All of this indicates that man has sensed always that wholeness or integrity is an absolute necessity to make life worth living.

—DAVID BOHM, WHOLENESS AND THE IMPLICATE ORDER, 1980

I think our capacity for wholeheartedness can never be greater than our willingness to be brokenhearted. It means engaging with the world from a place of vulnerability and worthiness.

—BRENÉ BROWN

Now he has departed from this strange world a little ahead of me. That means nothing. People like us, who believe in physics, know that the distinction between past, present, and future is only a stubbornly persistent illusion. —ALBERT EINSTEIN

The amazing stories of Sheila, Roger, and Marc prove that when you sense all of who you are, you realize you are more than your body, feelings, and thought. They offer you powerful demonstrations.

SHEILA'S STORY: RECEIVING A PERFECT HEALING MESSAGE

Sheila receives a RIM session as a gift for her fiftieth birthday, and she's curious to see what happens. When asked if there is anything that spontaneously comes to mind of what may be helpful to share before we start, her eyes tear up. Ten years ago Christmas Eve, her husband Phil died suddenly on their kitchen floor. She hasn't dated since his traumatic passing, though she feels lonely.

Sheila meditates regularly and finds it easy to follow her breath into deeper relaxation. Spontaneously, she senses herself walking on a beach. The softness of the sand is soothing to her feet. The sun warms her head as she hears the rhythmic sound of waves and she relaxes more. Out of the corner of her eye, she notices a figure in the distance. Intrigued, she watches the figure come closer and closer. It's her husband. She remarks: "He looks really different. In life, he was intense and demanding. Now, he's dressed in white, tan, and moving with ease. He's smiling and looks happy."

Sheila is taken aback by her dead husband's presence and senses his words:

Sheila, I know I didn't show it, but I really love you. I'm so sorry I was difficult; it wasn't because of you, you were wonderful. I was discontent with myself because I wasn't living up to my family's expectations for success. I felt inadequate, and I took it out on you. Please forgive me. My only remaining sadness is that my death has caused you pain and you remain lonely. I want you to fall in love again and have another relationship. Your happiness will complete my happiness.

As Sheila receives everything Phil has expressed, imagining it to be a stream of colored energy, a beautiful beam of white energy fills her. She reflects:

Phil, I hear you saying you loved me and your irritability wasn't my fault. Now that you are gone, it will complete your happiness if I go on with my life and create another loving relationship. Hearing you, Phil, is like having a weight lifted from my shoulders. I don't think I ever came out of the shock of seeing your body on our floor. It feels like I've been frozen in a bad dream for ten years. I am so grateful for your love and your unselfish wish for me to be happy in a new relationship. I feel free for the first time since that Christmas Eve. Thank you, Phil, I will never forget you.

When Sheila finishes, she and Phil hug. As this final embrace feels complete, a smiling Phil gradually becomes transparent and eventually fades away. As she looks through imagination to her body for where she's been carrying this grief, she gasps: "Oh my, it is my skin. All my skin is black. I've been wearing this grief as my skin!" Moving her attention to her skin, she instantly shares:

It's changing right before my eyes. It's turning into vivid murals of life everywhere on my skin. All the blackness is gone. There are people and plants, and the sun and life are thriving everywhere. My skin is living fully. It feels so good. So vibrant and alive!

Sheila loves her birthday present, and one month later she goes on her first date. A year later, she's in a long-term, committed relationship that continues to this day. Sheila received a perfect healing message without having asked for it. Something in her presence created a healing more profound than she could have thought possible.

ROGER'S STORY: UNRAVELING OLD SECRETS REVEALS NEW INSIGHTS

Roger is a bright and successful young man. In his thirties with a wife and family, he seems to have the golden touch, and his financial ventures are extremely successful. In fact, he's recently netted millions with the sale of a business. Yet he has a secret that bothers him, and he cannot get it out of his mind. Scheduling a session, he's too embarrassed to share, so he vaguely explains he's heard great things about RIM from his peers and wants to see what happens.

Beginning without a stated intention, Roger closes his eyes and scans his body to sense what is calling for his attention. There is a feeling in his heart area—he describes it as tightness. Identifying the tightness as a red sphere the size of a grapefruit with a smooth, dry surface, he gently moves his attention into it and immediately begins to feel intense anxiety. Asked for a spontaneous number from his imagination, Roger responds with "three," and the representative impression that pops up is a vivid image of three-year-old Roger lying in bed with his sleeping older brother; little Roger is intensely alert.

The movie that has haunted Roger for thirty years replays. His drunken father arrives home and stumbles into the boys' bedroom. As dad sits next to him, little Roger feels inquisitive and excited. This degree of attention from his father is unusual, and he is intrigued. Dad leans across to kiss Roger, but almost passes out, gets up, and walks out of the room. Roger is disappointed because nothing happened. He was so curious—there was such anticipation in his body.

There arises in his adult self a questioning: "What did little Roger want to happen? Why was he disappointed? Dad's drunken behavior is understood, but what of little Roger? Did he want something sexually inappropriate?" The adult Roger who understands sexual abuse is worried—does he have a problem?

As Roger calls for a virtual mentor to answer his question, a guardian angel named "Sarah" appears in his mind. She has shown up before in his meditations, but this is the first time he senses her name. "Why was I so curious, so excited?" he asks Sarah.

Feeling immense love from Sarah, Roger senses her answer:

Three-year-olds are extremely curious, Roger—that's all. Because your dad was gone so much of the time, of course you wanted to have an intimate moment with him. All children like to have their parent's single attention; it wasn't sexual. Roger, you are a healthy and wonderful man. You are a good father and husband. You deserve to thrive in every way. It's time, Roger, to forgive yourself; after all, you've already forgiven your father.

Upon receiving Sarah's message, Roger tearfully embraces his curious three-year-old self with forgiveness.

When Roger returns his attention to his body, there is more. A medium-gray energy pervades his gut; he finds it throughout his belly, and it feels quite uncomfortable, even nauseating, so much so that he is afraid he might vomit.

He describes the details of the energy: he senses a smooth, dry texture and solidity throughout. At the same time, there is intense anxiety in his heart. He scans his body and recognizes the gray energy in his gut is calling his attention most intently, and so he focuses on it. Bringing along angel Sarah for safety, Roger moves his attention into this unknown energy.

In the center appears a faint image of Roger's grown brother and his eighteen-month-old daughter. Exploring the scene, Roger becomes aware of a buried fear that his niece could be sexually abused by her dad because his brother "drinks every weekend." As Roger sees these images, he realizes this concern has been the source of his intense criticism of his brother's drinking; it has caused a great emotional distance between them, and Roger is aware that these feelings have kept him from spending time with his brother. He has not understood till now how these feelings are left over from the memory of his drunken father.

As adult Roger willingly speaks aloud to the image of his brother, a new insight emerges—his brother does not actually get drunk, he merely "drinks some beers." Roger's imagination has been confusing the truth with his own fears. In this imagined dialogue, Roger apologizes to his brother for misplacing his fears in their relationship. More tears of forgiveness arrive; the emotion is palpable as the two brothers unite in a forgiving and loving embrace.

After the session, Roger is astounded. First, he is shocked his secret has shown up organically without his naming it beforehand. Also, he's amazed to uncover how this aberrant memory has been creating unacknowledged emotional distance with his brother. The gratitude on his face is bright and his mood elated. Roger's story demonstrates how stuck feelings create intense physical discomfort. Furthermore, he could access wisdom greater than his human fears. We see in Roger the amazing power of the unconscious to reveal what's happening and why and resolve it in a quick, clear way.

MARC'S STORY: CALLING ON OUR EXTRAORDINARY ORGANIC RESOURCES

Marc has been working for four years in a high-security-level government job that he lucked into after graduating from college. He's proved himself an exceptional asset to his doctoral-level teammates because his thinking is fresh and out-of-the-box—the by-product of youthful desire to find new ways to do things. Some of his suggestions are so effective they've been adopted by Congress.

It's been a great ride for a young person, and now he's ready for something more or different. He decides to go for a graduate degree. Returning to the life of a full-time student is highly attractive both socially as well as career-wise.

His eye is on Harvard, but to his great disappointment, his application is rejected. On the other hand, he is accepted at the Johns Hopkins international program, which includes a nice financial package. It's a great school, but not exactly what he wants. He considers whether to accept the Hopkins offer or to delay a year and reapply to Harvard, but waiting another year to experience a second rejection is extremely unappealing. He's stuck in indecision, and the pressure is on because his work is sending him on a six-month assignment to Iraq. If he attends Hopkins, he must turn down the overseas assignment and start school within three months.

As he closes his eyes, his attention settles down into his body and he senses a heaviness in the bottom of his stomach. It feels black, rigid, unmoving, and very uncomfortable. The lack of movement calls his attention most intensely, so he shifts his awareness into the immobility and feels weighted down as though there are a thousand pounds on him. As he allows this feeling, he calls in someone to be with him—someone who is wise, powerful, and safe.

His imagination senses a tan, shaman-looking man walking down a mountain toward Marc. He doesn't know this man, so he asks for a name. "Antonio" is what pops into Marc's mind. Although he doesn't understand why, Marc feels good in Antonio's presence. There's something comforting about him, and as he accompanies Marc into the belly heaviness, something relaxes.

Marc senses Antonio inviting him to walk up the mountain with him, and he agrees. Being an outdoor kind of guy, walking with Antonio relaxes Marc further. It feels really good in fact.

They walk in silence for a while, noticing the comfort of nature. Then Antonio speaks:

Marc, you don't need to settle. Follow your intuition and apply to Harvard again next year. There's something in you that knows it will turn out. If you go to Hopkins, you can't go wrong, as it's a great school; however, your feeling of not being quite good enough to live your dreams will be reinforced—that's not true and unnecessary. You are good enough to fulfill your greatest dreams, Marc, and I'm here to remind you and support you to do that.

Marc receives all Antonio has expressed into his body like a stream of brilliant white energy, and his body responds. He now feels light and inspired. The old feeling of not being good enough evaporates, and Marc looks into Antonio's eyes—there is an affectionate exchange between them that feels exceptionally nourishing to Marc:

I'm so grateful for your belief in me, Antonio. It makes a big difference to me, and suddenly, I feel ready to go for it. It's kind of weird because I know you are just in my head, but you feel so real, I can't help but believe you. You feel more real than the Harvard rejection letter and that feels important.

Marc says no to the Hopkins offer and travels to Iraq where he works for six months and saves thirty thousand dollars for tuition because he's paid extra for a dangerous assignment. When he returns stateside, the timing is perfect to reapply to Harvard. Interestingly, his powerful Iraq experience becomes a key essay on his application, and Marc is ultimately accepted. It is a great day! He listened to Antonio, who spoke for Marc's heart, and it has all worked out well.

Now, he relaxes and calls up an image of Antonio whenever he needs help with confidence and decisions. This virtual mentor is always available with a smiling face and twinkling eyes. Marc finds it a different kind of relationship from talking in person to his family or friends. Antonio is connected to a wiser awareness within Marc, which feels really reliable and powerful.

Antonio shows us that we have organic resources beyond anything we have imagined in the rational world. Inner resources are easily available when we close our eyes, ask, listen, and act.

HOW IT WORKS—PRACTICALLY AND SCIENTIFICALLY

Aristotle wrote eight books collectively known as *Physics.* He is the source of the phrase "The whole is greater than the sum of its parts." In general, the phrase is interpreted as "The interaction of elements when combined produces a total effect that is greater than the sum of the individual elements, contributions, etc."[1]

Similarly, I've learned that we are more than our bodies, our brains, and our feelings. What we call our spirit, which we perceive virtually, holds the power to connect, communicate, and heal in ways not understood by our logical minds. This chapter explores how all human beings are whole in a way greater than the sum of their human parts. The remembrance of this inherent state of mind manifests outcomes that exceed what we've thought possible!

You Are So Much More than Your Physical Self

Who are you? What makes you "you" besides the color of your hair, your size, your shape, the design of your face, the three pounds of uniquely diverse microbes that inhabit your gut, the three pounds of unique brain cells that rest on your shoulders, the five liters of blood, the ten liters of interstitial fluid, and the 60 percent water weight that hydrates your body?

Science and culture focus primarily on what is material and visible because it's measurable, which has facilitated great scientific advances. However, when you ponder who "you" are, it doesn't ring true to reduce yourself to your body. It's a narrow perspective revealing a degenerative course of aging and physical death. You are more—don't you agree?

There is a quality within you that is indefinable. We named it in chapter two:

> We are more than our human thoughts and feelings. There is something in us that is so much more than our human condition, yet it is hard to put into words. It is the inner feeling you've had since you were a child . . . the feeling of being special . . . the feeling of being born for a reason (even if you do not know what it is), which, at the risk of sounding arrogant, you may not talk about and may even forget. This same awareness intuitively senses the purity and innocence of babies, the profundity of love, and the indescribable beauty of nature. It creates warm feelings in your body when you hold hands with someone you love, and it senses something greater when you look in the eyes of another human being and see that person's soul. For the sake of simplicity, we will call it human spirit, the intelligence of life itself that expresses as pure awareness and senses there is more to you than mere humanity.

Whether you call this subjective sense "self-awareness," "consciousness," "spirit," "soul," or something else, we all have it. I'll use the word *presence* to describe that aspect of you that is unlimited by space and time, which knows things you haven't studied, attracts serendipity, and makes you feel fully alive when embraced. Thank goodness there is more to you than your body, mind, and psychology, all of which have limitations. Unlimited presence is embodied in your unique physical structure. In other words, body, mind, and spirit blend to make you whole. No matter how you look at it, you are both humanity and presence.

It seems to me that some of us are born body-centered, while others are presence-centered. As we embrace our primary nature fully, life pushes us to expand in the opposite direction. Those of us attuned to presence are pushed to embrace our humanity, and those of us more in our bodies are urged to welcome presence.

I'm someone who's been more aware of spirit than body. At nine years old, I dreamily walked into a light pole and was almost knocked out. Other similar experiences followed. My craving of contemplative time much of my adult life was eventually satiated with two month-long meditation retreats to India. Contrary to my expectations, I returned home more embodied or more aware of my physical self and humanity. I've found I've grown more compassionate and better able to get things done in the world as a result. I've also run out of gas or gotten lost less often, which is convenient.

Those naturally more in touch with their physical nature have a different course. A client named Allie recently experienced going back to first grade, where she felt restrained to her desk. Experiencing the world primarily through her body and without words, it felt torturous to sit quietly and listen to her first-grade teacher. Because her inherent urge to move was interrupted, she developed a body memory of not being in touch with herself and being different from the attentive first-graders sitting around her. She's had repeated experiences of feeling she's not like other people.

When Allie regenerated her first-grade memory, she freely left the classroom and spent the day on the playground accompanied by her mother who "understood me because she's similar." Letting her body move freely, Allie began to feel like herself. As she moved and danced and skipped, she sensed her "inner light radiating." Embracing the inherent body-centeredness of the first-grader stimulated a greater awareness of her presence.

Some people push their bodies to run harder, bike further, and ski faster. When health and other issues temper that physical excelling, changes deepen an appreciation for presence, resulting in greater connection with self and others.

Wholeness comes with the acknowledgment of who we are—all of us—the good, the bad, and the ugly. Embracing the combination of our humanity and presence enhances an unshakable feeling of "wholeness," or "integral, complete, unimpaired, perfect, undiminished totality."[2]

With your eyes closed, sense the number your imagination gives you between one and ten of how much you are embracing your body/humanity, with ten being the most. Circle it below.

| 1 | 2 | 3 | 4 | 5 | 6 | 7 | 8 | 9 | 10 |

With your eyes closed, sense the number your imagination gives you between one and ten of how much you are embracing your presence, with ten being the most. Circle it below.

| 1 | 2 | 3 | 4 | 5 | 6 | 7 | 8 | 9 | 10 |

Contemplate how this balance of humanity and presence shows up in your lifestyle and what value there is in allowing a greater appreciation for both your humanity and your presence. Completing the following sentences may be helpful:

How I feel when I embrace my humanity is . . .

How I feel when I embrace my presence is . . .

The unique benefits of embracing my humanity and presence more are . . .

The Power of Virtual Resources

As humans we sometimes feel separate and alone, but presence allows us to connect with others even when we are physically separated. As we learn to notice the always available emotional support, we gain a sense of resilience that transcends space and time and anchors in the body.

In the RIM process, inner safety is evoked by calling forth virtual resources. These imagined mentors feel real and elicit goose bumps. Imagination is asked to flash a spontaneous image of someone or something that is safe, loving, powerful, and wise. It can be quite surprising who shows up, as you saw when Sheila's husband appeared to heal her pain and the imaginary shaman Antonio guided Marc to trust himself. A sampling of the resources I've witnessed in client sessions over the last twenty years include God, Jesus, Buddha, Spirit, White Light, Mother Teresa, Gandhi, saints from various traditions, guardian angels, Santa, spirit guides, higher selves, grandparents, aunts, uncles, cousins, Mother Nature, pets alive or deceased, supportive friends/neighbors, and older, younger, and wiser selves. These figures provide a visceral sense of being loved rather than alone. Right now, close your eyes and imagine someone who loves you and notice how you feel. Take a minute to explore this awareness.

Contrary to traditional techniques where the therapist/counselor/coach is the safety figure, in RIM the client's virtual mentors are tapped to assure safety and expanded insight. Thus, the client is empowered by personal resources who are always available. You can try out sensing a unique virtual resource in the Practice It Yourself section.

Sarah Master of the University of California found that having someone with you can relieve the intensity of your physical pain. Interestingly, holding the photo of a significant other gave greater comfort than their actual presence.[3] This finding suggests that virtual support is more comforting than a real person and offers scientific support to why virtual resources work so effectively.

Sometimes people ask if these virtual resources are real or merely imaginary. I'm not sure, but I have discovered it doesn't matter. Based on their worldviews, some believe them to be real, while others do not. Either way, the virtual presence of a safe

and powerful resource is felt viscerally and creates an empowering memory regardless of what the intellect thinks. You saw this
in Marc's story, when he felt better with Antonio's words than
those of family and friends even though he considered Antonio
just imaginary. Scientific research shows that imagining a physical activity and physically executing it light up similarly on MRI
tests.[4] Thus, interacting with an imagined mentor is experienced
as real in emotional memory. Although the brain retains factual
awareness of what's real and what's imagined, emotional memory is more powerful in creating a felt-body experience of safety
and love.[5]

In Roger's real-life story, his adult self fears that his three-
year-old self is excited by the hint of a sexual connection with his
drunken father, but the guardian angel Sarah easily appears and
speaks to him with immense love to overcome this doubt. It's
easy for Roger to be comforted because her unconditional love
is palpable.

Similarly in Sheila's story, her husband's spirit emotionally
completes his relationship with her in a beautiful way, so she is
free to pursue other relationships. We have more resources than
we think; we merely have to close our eyes and imagine. Something inside us already knows what's needed and provides!

Since the client's imagination is in charge of creating the RIM
process (not the intellect), it reveals the unknown. In this virtual,
unlimited space, things are learned that are considered unknow-
able by the thinking mind. For example, the spirits of birth fathers
and mothers who died or left when their children were young can
be sensed and known; this experience is life-changing. After such
a journey, people have said: "Now I know who I am" or "Now I
know why I am the way I am; I feel like I exist for the first time."
For example, when Allison requests a RIM process, she is feeling
frustrated there isn't more affection in her marriage. She doesn't
mention anything about her father. When she closes her eyes and

dips deeply into body sensations, her attention is drawn to her right eye and temple: "It's like there is a darkness on my upper right eye, like someone is there creating a shadow, but it's blurry and I can't make it out."

With encouragement Allison gives her complete attention to this shadowy figure. Completely engrossed in curiosity, she says: "It's still blurry, but it seems masculine. I think it's a man." Taking the time she needs, she stays with this image until she begins to cry: "It's so strange, but I sense this is my real father. I never knew him, so I don't know what he looks like, but it feels like this is a familiar male energy."

I ask if she wants to speak with him and she says yes. She shares with him:

I feel you are my father, although I never knew you. You feel so familiar, it makes me cry. I've wished to know you my whole life. Here you are and I can sense the warmth and smell of your body; it feels so comforting and substantial. I'm so happy to know you after all these forty-some years. At the same time, I'm afraid to ask you, but I have to, 'Why did you leave me?' You can't image all the scenarios I've imagined. Mom said you left and didn't give a reason. It feels like you didn't care enough to know me, that you didn't love me.

Moving into the shadowy figure of Dad, Allison senses his response by looking from his eyes:

Allison, I didn't know you because your mother never told me I had a daughter. She and I dated awhile and then we didn't. I didn't know you existed. I look at the lovely person you are and I realize how much I've missed by not being there as your father and I'm very sad. I regret that I didn't get to be there with you over the years and I promise to be there for you now through your imagination. I love you and want the best for you.

After Allison's experience with her dad, she says she feels different, like she owns her place in the world. Other fatherless/motherless and adopted clients have had similar experiences.

Loneliness Is a Perception

Existential loneliness has been explained by philosophers throughout history and felt by most of us at one time or another. During adolescence, when we are emancipating from our parents, we find we especially want to belong to a group; otherwise there's an uncomfortable feeling of separateness and rejection. Emotional and physical crises are other lonely times when being supported by a group makes us feel better.

Interestingly, being alone elicits different emotions depending on the circumstances. For example, loneliness implies wanting someone to be with us who is not. However, solitude is a desire to be alone. The key difference is whether we can have what we want or not. The suffering comes when we want to be with someone and feel we can't. We're more likely to want someone with us when we're feeling afraid and insecure.

Virtual resources allow free access to safe, loving, and powerful mentors at any time and place. Thus, the feeling of loneliness can evaporate instantly while confronting overwhelming feelings and difficult relationships, as you've read in the real-life stories. Over the last twenty years, I've been amazed at the power of virtual resources not only to distill loneliness, but also to bring extraordinary guidance and love. As mentioned previously, the nervous system receives real and imagined experience similarly, though factual memory remains intact. Thus imagining a virtual mentor evokes a genuine feeling of being supported and loved. Frequently, people want to connect with a virtual resource daily for ongoing support. Common times chosen are on waking, going to bed, and during meditation.

Kurt is a forty-something doctor with a somewhat angry attitude because his dad left the family when Kurt was a boy and never supported them emotionally or financially. Fortunately, his mom filled both parental roles.

When Kurt dips into body sensing during a session, he discovers his eleven-year-old self. Although his dad isn't available emotionally or physically, Kurt is free to expresses intense hurt and anger directly to him. Afterward, Kurt's virtual mentor Jesus says:

> Kurt, you are brave to speak honestly with your dad. Although he isn't mature enough to be a parent to you, you are loved more than any human love. I love you, and I'm always with you without the distractions of humanity. Continue to open your heart to this immense and infinite fatherly love; it's always available. You merely need to listen.

Kurt receives what Jesus has expressed like a blinding light in his throat, radiating throughout his body. Light spins in his torso and projects him and Jesus into outer space. Floating in the universe with the stars and planets, he is transported into a state of stillness he's never experienced before. As they glide through the stars, he feels a sense of connectedness to all life. His awareness of his body fades, and he receives glimmers of the wisdom of the ages. Kurt is here as long as he wants. As this timeless moment is culminating, he glimpses earth and senses his human life. From this perspective, he knows that all that's happened has prepared him to be a compassionate and effective healer. In this way, Kurt's dad is playing his role perfectly, and Kurt feels grateful for his life just the way it was, is, and will be. Feelings of blame turn to gratitude and he is ready to return to his body and the room. Two years later I run into him, and he shares, "I've never forgotten that moment I floated in space. It's still real."

I recently saw a report on television of the results of a research project from the University of Calgary where children undergoing medical procedures were provided with small personal robots to verbally interact with and support them. It reminds me of the extraordinary power of virtual resources. We can feel less alone by connecting with many kinds of resources. We have more resources than we've thought; it just looks different from what we've expected.

Revealers of Expanded Insight and Intelligence

You have probably noticed that virtual resources in the real-life stories we've looked at are able to share different perspectives on the issues at hand. They introduce a significantly wiser voice than the client's. For example, Louise is a college professor in her sixties. Her outward appearance is conservative, intelligent, and a bit timid. Attending a business seminar, she becomes agitated and complains to the staff that people in the room are spraying her with toxins. Speaking with her and her psychiatrist, I learn she has been diagnosed with paranoia, medicated, and not dangerous, so we decide to let her stay in the program, provided she doesn't disrupt others. When she asks for a RIM session, I'm surprised. She explains that she has sensed a heavy concrete slab on her chest during the group RIM process and wants to get rid of it.

As she closes her eyes, her sense of the heaviness is palpable. When she moves her attention into it, I suggest that her imagination bring her an image of a safe and loving virtual mentor who wants to walk her through this journey. Immediately, a favorite aunt who has passed away appears, and Louise is quick to comment that this aunt always liked her. This appreciation seems important since Louise is recently divorced and her adult son hasn't talked to her for eight months. She quickly feels safe, and we proceed to ask her aunt to voice what wants to be said. Moving attention into her aunt, Louise speaks for her:

Louise, I know you feel afraid, but these people [those she imagines are tormenting her] aren't going to hurt you. They'll eventually go away. Until then, don't let them upset you. If they eat your food, buy more, and if they mess up your house, pay someone to clean it. They won't harm you, I promise, and you don't need to waste your energy on them.

Louise immediately heeds her aunt's words. After this interaction, the heaviness is gone, and she feels safer and calmer. Louise agrees with the suggestion that she connect daily with her aunt, and we're done in thirty minutes. When I follow up several months later, she is doing well. She acknowledges the continuing connection with her aunt's voice has been extremely helpful and comforting.

As a mental health professional who has worked in inpatient psychiatry, I was surprised to learn Louise could trust her aunt. Apparently, there is a virtual place in paranoia where she could connect without fear. Louise's story reminds me of our inner resourcefulness in spite of mental illness as demonstrated in *A Beautiful Mind,* the 1998 book and Oscar-winning movie about the life of John Nash, Nobel laureate in economics. Although he suffered with paranoid schizophrenia, he consciously learned to disarm the delusional images and fears so he could live a productive life.

The range of wisdom that shows up through virtual mentors and intuition is quite extraordinary—beyond anything the conscious minds of the client or facilitator could conjure. For example, Anita, a physician who has been divorced for six years, is obsessed with thoughts about her ex-husband. Her intellectual mind knows the separation was the right decision, and she's extremely mad at herself for not being able to move on. Although an issue with her husband seems to be the problem, her process reveals that the root cause goes deeper.

Initially Anita senses a grinding feeling in her jaws. This tight energy is dense, menacing, and heavy. As Anita moves into this energy, an image of her mother and twenty-five-year-old self appears. She's angry her mom doesn't support her competency, independence, and desire to become a doctor. Her stay-at-home mom can't engage with her dreams, and Anita calls in a virtual resource for help. The Archangel Michael appears with huge, white wings and offers them both protection.

With a new feeling of safety, Anita freely expresses what is in her heart without fear of hurting her mom. She then senses a "second-guessing feeling" in her chest that takes Anita into an issue more deeply hidden. It looks like blue-green energy, and when she goes into it, a four-foot silver sword with five feet of gray fog is revealed. With Michael for protection, she moves into the fog and senses that it's there to keep her from going too far; it regulates her so she doesn't "do something stupid." When she asks the fog for the source of this fear, it responds that something happened in medical school.

Anita recalls the terrible event and immediately begins to cry. Something went wrong and the patient died. Calling up an image of the patient's spirit, Anita sheepishly sinks into her chair and tearfully speaks to him: "I'm sorry, Mr. Sanders, I was learning, and I probably tried to do too much too soon. I feel terrible."

Mr. Sanders' spirit receives her words like a bluish-white energy and she senses his response: "It was worse for you than me. It wasn't that big a deal because I was dying anyway. Actually you saved me further pain and turmoil in the process. I hope you let this go and enjoy your life."

Anita receives his words like red energy that turns white as it fills her heart. She is amazed by the palpable feeling of his spirit in the room—his warmth and energy. Comforted, she feels "lifted up out of a hole."

Anita's journey is layered. Initially it seems Anita's ex-husband is the culprit, then her mom presents as a hindrance to her being heard and supported. Eventually, internal images uncover the source traumatic event—a fatal medical incident that made her question her judgment.

After this RIM experience, Anita's obsession with her ex-husband is completely gone. She trusts herself to live without his control. He had matched her hidden insecurity by demanding their life be all about him and his needs, which kept her from testing out her independence and making fatal mistakes. Even after they divorced and she was surviving without him, the deeply buried pain of the mistake lingered in her subconscious and held her back. During this experience, her presence adeptly uncovered the root event and brought resolution. Through imagination, she dissolved her guilt and regained a deep sense of self-trust.

Inner Safety

Researcher Bessel Van Der Kolk explains that the seat of primitive human reaction lies in the lower reptilian brain. He calls it the smoke detector because it sounds our danger alarm when we're threatened. The neocortex sits high in the brain and allows an elevated awareness. Van Der Kolk calls this the watchtower—that area of the brain where mindfulness awakens the centering, calming function.[6]

The safety and love of virtual resources simultaneously defuse the emotional smoke detector and activate the mindful watchtower. Although simple, the effect of virtual resources yields profound benefits as you've witnessed in the real-life stories.

Our inner resourcefulness defies the limits of physical reality. For example, a woman who was neglected by her Korean father, raped as a young adult, and employed as a prostitute for a few years has difficulty sensing a virtual mentor because of intense and justified mistrust of others. When asked what in nature could provide safety, she gets a spontaneous and vivid image of a beautiful field of flowers. Her presence immediately softens, and her mouth reflexively smiles. Standing in the center of the flowers, she feels absolutely safe—enough to express her anger with her father. During this dialogue, she learns he always loved her yet felt inept interacting with a girl because in Korea it wasn't customary for a father to be close to his daughters. This revelation transforms the way she sees herself and how she interacts with men. No longer feeling "they are just out to take advantage," she is able to interact in an adult, discerning way.

Who would have thought first of all that a field of flowers could keep this woman safe, or second, that her father's emotional distance was so easily explained? This elevated level of awareness is astounding and can flip stuck painful injury immediately in pervasive ways.

PRACTICE IT YOURSELF

Calling Forth a Virtual Resource Activity

You may have experienced a connection with a virtual resource— or this may be your first opportunity. Either way, you'll get the best results if you relax your body and your expectations. Rest in a state of curiosity with a willingness to notice what flashes into your mind first, regardless of its form. It may not make sense initially, or you may be tempted to edit, but just trust what comes. Again, you may see, hear, feel, or sense images, so remember this is more than a visual activity; it is multisensory and evocative. Have a paper and pen available in case you want to record anything during the process.

- Listen to soft music to help you relax as you focus your attention inside your body.

- Sensing the center of your body, notice what it's like here. As you take four deep breaths, your imagination calls up the image of a virtual resource: it could be a wise ancestor, guardian angel, a deity of your faith, an animal, or any-one or anything that's loving, powerful, and safe. Receiv-ing who/what pops into your awareness first, sense the details, e.g., color, size, clothes, location in relationship to you, etc. Take whatever time you need or want.

- Moving into the virtual resource, look from its eyes at yourself and notice how you look and act and sound. Take a minute.

- Sense what the virtual resource wants to say to you, and write or speak these words from the virtual resource to you.

- Continuing to look out of the eyes/perspective of the vir-tual mentor, complete the following sentence leads spo-ken by this individual to you:

  - What I know about you and your purpose, (*your name*), is . . .

  - What I sense about your talents that you haven't noticed is . . .

  - What is wanting to express through you is . . .

  - What you are pretending not to know is . . .

  - Above all else, what you need to know is . . .

  - What I love most about you is . . .

- Insert here specific questions for the virtual resource to answer. Again sense the response by looking through the eyes of the virtual resource at yourself.

- Moving your awareness back into yourself, imagine receiv-ing everything the resource has expressed like a stream of colored energy flowing into you. Notice the color and quality of this stream and where it enters your body.

- When you are done, record your experience on paper.

Who am I? asks my Soul
Heaven and Earth, whispers the wind
You are stardust, bone, and sinew
Enlivened with Presence
Is that not enough?
Yes, resounds Life

REPEL & ATTRACT

Your Feelings Are Magnetic

Magnetism is one of the six fundamental forces of the Universe, with the other five being gravity, duct tape, whining, remote control, and the force that pulls dogs toward the groins of strangers.

—DAVE BARRY

Now if this electron is displaced from its equilibrium position, a force that is directly proportional to the displacement restores it like a pendulum to its position of rest.

—PETER ZEEMAN

When you emotionally flip magnetic memory, you repel misfortune and attract good luck and good health. The ability to dissolve the hidden influence of forgotten experience is empowering beyond what we've thought possible. Tom, Heather, and Craig have enacted it in real life. Their stories will amaze you.

TOM'S STORY: EARLY EMOTIONAL CONFLICTS ATTRACT MORE OF THE SAME

Tom has been home from Afghanistan for almost a year, but his feelings of shame continue. It shows subtly in the way he lowers his head and sucks in his chest. He feels like a failure—there's no pride in having served his country.

When Tom closes his eyes and focuses on his body, his heart draws his attention. It's dark with a leather casing. As he moves into it, he feels the toughness. His imagination calls up an image of the first time he felt this way, and Tom's dad comes into view. It's during high school when he and his dad are constantly at odds. A Lebanese emigrant with Eastern values, his dad believes strongly in humility. Tom, however, has grown up in the United States with Western values. He is the youngest son, and while his elder brother is quiet and shy, Tom loves attention. He is attractive, outgoing, and frequently the life of the party, which his dad judges poorly; this is not Dad's concept of a "good man," and he is determined his sons will be good men in spite of American values. The result is persistent conflict between them.

Tom volunteers for military service, and the emotional distance between them widens. He is sure if he is far away from his father's judgments, he can demonstrate his abilities and be a hero. However, he returns from the military ashamed and disappointed because he isn't a hero. In fact, he never saw battle. Now he wants to help vets, but feels embarrassed and diminished. No surprise, the vet assistance program he's launching is stalling.

Speaking from his high school self, Tom talks honestly to his Dad for the first time in his life:

Dad, you make me feel so bad. I don't think you know how much your judgments hurt. You make me feel like you don't like who I am and that you don't love me. Instead you prefer my brother because he's controllable. Yet, I'm different from him and you. In fact, my life has been very different from yours, and I can't fit into the mold of what you want without losing myself and my self-respect. It makes me really sad to feel so distant from you. I want us to be close and have fun together. I wish you could look at me and be proud. I feel I'm failing you, but I can't be someone else. I don't know what to do. It feels better to speak honestly rather than getting mad and rebelling. I miss having a dad.

Moving his attention into Dad and looking through this perspective, he speaks with the lead, "What I hear you saying, Tom, is . . .":

Tom, I hear you saying you feel judged and unloved, and though you want to be close, you feel I want you to be what I want rather than who you are. Oh, Tom, I had no idea you felt this way. I'm so sorry I've made you feel ashamed of who you are because you are different from your brother and me. I just wanted you to be a good man. I guess I still have a bit of my parents' thinking in my head. I recognize, Tom, I am old-fashioned in this contemporary American world. Tom, you are a good man. You are kind and sincere and I love you immensely—I always have. Please believe me. I want you to be happy with yourself and go out and follow your dreams. After all, following my dreams is what got us here in America in the first place. Hmm . . . maybe you are more like me than I've realized. I was ambitious and wanted to get away from the constrictions of my parents' world, too.

Tom moves back into himself and receives all his dad has said like a stream of colored energy. Tom speaks again:

Dad, I hear that you love me and you're sorry for judging me and that you want me to feel good being myself. I'm surprised, Dad, to hear that I am more like you than you or I realized.

Somehow that feels reassuring. I'm not as much of a family misfit as I've thought. Maybe, even, I'm normal.

Thank you, Dad, for apologizing, it means so much to me; it makes me feel grounded, like I can trust my own instincts. I also feel close to you through this conversation—a new feeling and I like it. I want to make you and me proud of the kind of person I am, and now I feel optimistic I can. I don't know what it looks like, but I feel empowered.

As this conversation comes to an end, Tom turns away from his dad to look at his Afghanistan experience. From this new perspective of feeling loved, Tom watches a review of his military tour on the screen of his mind. When asked how this experience looks now, Tom replies:

Wow! It looks very normal. I see myself being a good soldier who is supportive of the other men in my troop. It seems unimportant that I returned without medals or fanfare. Rather, the focus is that I have a happy life and this great opportunity to help vets who need it. I feel confident.

Finding the feeling of confidence in his body, Tom identifies it as a bright, orange energy suffusing him. He imagines becoming one with the orange energy, which heightens the feeling and anchors it in memory.

Tom's war experience is an emotional repetition of feeling like a failure. When he resolves the original "failure" with his dad, the Afghanistan tour automatically transforms and his angst disappears. He organically regains his acceptance of himself. Other vets who have returned home traumatized have also gone back via RIM to an original conflict with their fathers.

Tom's story demonstrates how early emotional conflicts attract similar feelings until they are resolved at their origin. This attraction is dissolved quickly once the root cause is revealed and deconstructed.

HEATHER'S STORY: THE DEPTH OF HEALING IS PROPORTIONAL TO THE DEGREE OF PAIN

Heather is in her early thirties and working in the IT department of a large computer company. She's unhappy with her life and constantly parties and sleeps around. Her hair, skin, and eyes look dull, and her persona subtly expresses a cynical perspective as if she expects life to dump on her, so she'll maintain control by dumping on herself first.

As Heather engages in multiple RIM sessions, she processes several "I've been done wrong" experiences with boyfriends and coworkers. After each session, she feels lighter and more respectful of herself, and there is a progression toward more highly charged events. In high school she is seduced by a much older boyfriend who demands sex and lots of it or else he will leave. She doesn't want to, but acquiesces because she doesn't want to lose him. Then he suddenly drops her without any explanation. The intense pain dissolves during a session as she stands up to him and claims her voice. Afterward, she feels a big lift in mood and empowerment, and her friends are inquiring about what she's doing differently because she's looking attractive in a new way.

The original magnetic experience eventually surfaces when her inner body sensations guide her to her dad. As she relaxes, she notices a feeling of heaviness in her gut; as she moves into it, her imagination projects the source scene of her dad angrily yelling: "You are a slut." He has discovered she's sleeping with the demanding boyfriend and he's out-of-control furious. He's been emotionally absent and spends his free time with his son doing guy-things like hunting. Unfortunately, her first father-daughter connection is imprinted with pain. Since her mother is busy with home and work, she hasn't engaged with Heather either, and Heather realizes she's never felt cherished except by the boyfriend. She has been repeatedly feeling and acting as if she is "damaged goods" and unworthy of positive attention until this demagnetizing experience.

By this time, Heather's dad has died, so we call in his "passed-over spirit" to be there with her projection of the living human dad in this scene. Interestingly, imagination consistently reflects one's passed-over spirit as wiser than one's human self. With the support of her virtual resource she identifies as "Granny," high school Heather speaks angrily:

> You have no right to say anything to me because you've never been here as my father. You were off doing what you wanted with my brother. You never even talked to me. You made me feel as if being a girl meant I was nothing. The reason I would do anything to keep a boyfriend, even have sex when I didn't want to, is because he gave me attention and made time for me. For a while I was the center of his attention, and it felt so good because I've never had that from you or Mom. It feels like you don't love me, especially when you call me despicable names. I don't feel loved or even respected by you.

As she looks over at images of human and spirit Dad, Heather sees both receive all that she's said like a stream of colored energy. When that's complete, she sees it's spirit Dad who wants to respond, and she moves her attention to look out of his eyes, sense what he wants to say, and speak for him:

> You are right, Heather, and I'm so sorry. I can see now how unfair I was to you and how I ignored you. I didn't know how to father a daughter. I thought of you as my little princess, and I didn't realize it wasn't obvious. I grew up with brothers, and I'm not comfortable with girls. I thought your mom could teach you better than me. Now I understand I was very wrong, and I want you to know I love you very much and always have. Even when I was angry, I still loved you. When I called you a slut, it wasn't because of you, it was my anger being out of control and

I'm sorry. Can you ever forgive me? If I had it to do over, I'd
be different. I'd put time into our relationship and also into the
relationship with your mom, because I ignored her also. I see
things much clearer now.

Heather receives all that's been expressed like a stream of colored energy and speaks again:

Dad, I hear you say you loved me and you'd do it differently
if you had the chance. I never thought I'd hear that from you,
and it makes me feel so much better. I felt that if my own dad
couldn't love me, I must be unlovable. I'm sensing how important your love is to me. I feel lighter and more worthy. It sounds
strange, yet life seems simpler all of a sudden. Like I can imagine
being successful and feeling satisfied.

When Heather and her dad are asked if they'd like to regenerate a new history, both enthusiastically agree. Virtual resource
Granny rewinds the scene and pauses at the perfect moment to
create something new. As the new memory is created through
imagination, Heather and Dad witness themselves being buddies
with special times together. Dad shows his love for her, and it's
quite beautiful. Heather cherishes the feeling of it! The movie
integrates in her gut and around her like a soft, comforting blanket, so she can sense it constantly.

Within months, Heather is promoted and receives a big raise.
She looks like a different woman from the one who originally
walked in the door. She has bright eyes and skin and flashes a
radiant smile.

Heather's journey demonstrates how the depth of healing is
proportional to the degree of pain. Regenerating the most painful experience will produce the greatest positive outcome. The
wholeness of her presence remained beneath the deepest wound
and automatically surfaced after numerous layers of healing
allowed her to address the relationship with her dad.

CRAIG'S STORY: NO LONGER "DEFECTIVE"

Craig comes from a Jewish family and is the youngest of three siblings. When his parents divorced, he became the object of his siblings' anger while both parents were preoccupied.

Craig has since become a lawyer. He's happily married and living a good life, but he notices his aggressive feelings toward their dogs when they misbehave and strangely senses an undercurrent of rage. It shows up most when strangers are rude, and he responds excessively. Careful to contain the feelings, he's afraid of what might happen if he doesn't restrain himself.

As Craig begins his session, it's his brain that first calls his attention. It seems flesh-colored and convoluted like a typical picture of a brain. As he moves into this image with the suggestion, "You'll sense an image of the source of this feeling," his little boy face with pink cheeks and freckles pops into awareness. Becoming little Craig, he feels a tinge of anger as he looks from his young eyes. He immediately sees his older teenage sister. In reality, she passed away in the sixties due to drug and alcohol use.

Asking for a virtual resource to appear, Craig is joined by dear friend and business mentor Peter, who stands between little Craig and his sister as his younger self says:

> You're pretty great to see, Sis, because it's scary with what's going on with Mom and Dad. I know this yelling you've been doing is because you are rejected and abused by our father. However, I don't see any reason for you to abuse me. I'm not the cause of this. What you're doing to me is unacceptable. As a little boy, I feel hurt and angry about it.

The voice of adult Craig gives a historical perspective: "I've wasted so many years as if I were defective. It was very cruel the way you laughed at my expense. It was unfair." Behind his ribs, Craig senses an image of a black football, and he moves into that and speaks: "I'm not going to hit you, though there's no one to protect you, but I feel like it."

When he's given permission to express his anger physically in the scene, he imagines smashing a softball into the couch. He also smashes eggs and feels the coldness of the yolk running all over. He looks over at his sister and sees her sadness and confusion.

Moving his attention into her, he senses her receiving all little Craig has expressed like a stream of colored energy. Looking through her eyes, he speaks what she wants to say:

> Craig, I owe you a gigantic apology. I was out of control. Craig, you are fine as you are. What I did and said to you was unfair and abusive. I never knew you felt this. I'm sorry. I'm shocked to hear all of this. I'm sorry neither of us developed enough to sit down and have an honest talk. You were just a little boy. If I'd had more maturity, I would have listened to you.

We call forth the sister's passed-over spirit to support her teen self. Now the spirit speaks to her younger self: "Let me hold you and squeeze you with love. You were the oldest and over your head. You were asked to carry the emotional weight. It feels good to be able to acknowledge you finally."

Teen sister receives all the love from her passed spirit—it appears like a pink ballet energy. As she fully receives it, she feels pain-free, lighthearted, and dancing gracefully like a ballerina.

Little Craig speaks again to his sister: "I love you very, very much. I have sadness that you're not around. I wish you love and joy. Now I know the truth of why you said those things to me, and I'm glad you're in a happy place now." With this sharing, Craig feels peace in his stomach and tears on his cheeks. He senses lightness in his body.

He experiences great benefits from this session and wants a second session to work with his brother. Although he's participated in psychotherapy previously, the experience of sensing the charge in his body, speaking directly to his sister, and sensing her response is profoundly different.

As Craig closes his eyes, he notices a large white oval plate rotating counterclockwise behind his eyes. Moving into this image, he senses a feeling of "being invisible to assure safety." This thought incites feelings of rage, and his virtual mentor Peter returns to instill calming.

An image of Craig's older brother also shows up. When asked who speaks first, it's the brother:

> I see you are more loving and compassionate with Dad than I am, and there's a part of me that's jealous. The way our father is walking out is a bunch of crap. We're being robbed of our childhood, and I'm really angry and hurt. You don't seem to get it. You're always smiling, and I just want to kill you. If you joined me in showing anger with Dad, that would help. You're a pussy, but I'm a very angry boy, and I don't care.

Craig senses his brother's rage—a "red ball like a sun demon." As he moves into the ball for his brother, he speaks for him to their dad:

> Dad, you can't fucking abandon your children. You don't even look at me, and you don't tell us goodbye. It's been horrible. I'm so angry, and I'm especially upset I've turned into you—clinical and cold—because of your lack of physical touch.

A virtual resource is called forth for Craig's brother. Cousin Mike appears and decides to put the rage (red ball) into an atomic bomb and explode it safely. Craig's brother feels accepted now and turns to talk to little Craig:

> I need you to stand up to me. Be equal to me. I was more concerned about myself. I love you, Craig, and I was afraid my anger might hurt you. I was a nutcase and feel relieved to get in touch with the rage and express it. I'm so intellectually smart, it's easy

for me to feel above it, yet it's been there. As I become aware of these feelings, I feel sad and tears are coming. This could be the beginning of a friendship between us, Craig.

Little Craig responds: "I'm glad you knew I was a scared little boy and that you know you use your intellect to distance. It feels good to hear you say it." As Craig senses his body, it feels different: "Now there's an unconstrained feeling, like my blood is flowing freely, a thunderstorm has moved away, and there's blue sky."

Craig reports later he now feels taller, stronger, and more confident. His old complaints of feeling "defective" are gone. His story demonstrates how we can neutralize complicated painful relationships without actual conversation with those involved, including virtually blowing up his brother's rage. The power is within us.

HOW IT WORKS—PRACTICALLY AND SCIENTIFICALLY

In the same way a magnet creates an invisible field that attracts ferrous material, highly charged emotion has a strong subconscious force field that attracts similar feelings and repels opposite ones. Researcher Candace Pert discovered that we have mood-specific receptor sites in the nervous system; some are attracted to pleasure while others to pain. Once they are in place, she suggests these are the molecules of emotion that can attract or repel specific emotions.[1]

Robert M. Sapolsky, professor of biology and neurology at Stanford University, further demonstrates how the repeated firing of emotion-specific neurons causes them to become "hyperresponsive."[2] Thus, less and less stimulation is needed to prompt the same behavior that elicits the same feeling. In other words, the more you respond to your environment in the same emotional way, the more neurologically primed your body is to repeat this behavior automatically without your conscious agreement.

The landmark ACE (Adverse Childhood Experiences) Study by Kaiser found that early traumatic experience attracts similar adult experience. For example, women with childhood abuse and neglect are seven times more likely to be raped in adulthood. Similarly, women who witnessed their mothers being assaulted by their partners have a vastly increased chance of falling into a relationship with domestic violence. Psychiatrist and researcher Bessel Van Der Kolk explains that "traumatized individuals can become too hypervigilant to enjoy the ordinary pleasures of life, and others may become too numb to absorb new experience or be alert to signs of real danger."[3]

Fortunately, recent neuroscience studies reveal the brain is "plastic" and always available to update and erase previous learning.[4] At the site of the original memory, we can dissolve old harmful images and generate empowered ones that attract healthy life patterns. It's like rewinding a movie to an influential scene that's been on permanent pause and recording over it with an empowered version.

This chapter demonstrates that we can dissolve painful/sabotaging memory to repel similar future experience, thereby attracting healthier outcomes.

Organically Uncovering the Magnetic Memory

If I ask you about the first time you fell in love, you could recall from factual memory your physical and emotional experience— this is explicit memory that's conscious and verbal. Implicit memory is not as easily tapped because it's unconscious and nonverbal, subtly imprinted in the body. To uncover implicit memory, you go back to an actual first love encounter and relive it. Implicit memory is embedded as sensory and emotional, while explicit memory contains both subjective, verbally accessible recall and factual memory.[5] Implicit memory has immensely greater magnetic charge to attract automatic repetition of an experience. Thus, it's what we seek to uncover and reconstruct to project a healthy future.

The good news is that Ecker, Ticic, and Hulley in their book *Unlocking the Emotional Brain* prove implicit emotional memory (subcortical and right-brain) can be converted to explicit memory. Furthermore, the authors explain: "Neuroscience research since 2004 has shown that the brain does indeed have a key to those locked synapses: a type of neuroplasticity . . . [that] unlocks the synapses of a target emotional learning, allowing it to be not merely overridden but actually nullified and deleted by new learning." They go on to say: "New learning always creates new neural circuits, but it is only when new learning also unwires old learning that transformational change occurs."[6]

We now understand that it is neurologically possible to bring unknown charged emotional events into conscious awareness and regenerate an empowering edition. These advances prove you can teach an old dog new tricks, and we old dogs are quite excited!

Locating a charged emotion with RIM is similar to using a magnetic locator. The mechanical tool senses magnetic fields of buried ferromagnetic objects like property markers, manholes, septic tanks, cast-iron pipes, and steel drums buried up to sixteen feet below the earth's surface. Similarly, we can search the body to find where magnetic emotional events are buried because they send out sensory messages. They organically defuse when uncovered and reworked.

Li Na's story demonstrates how the same principle also works in the material world. She's a Chinese Olympic tennis champion who hit a slump after her victory at the French Open in 2011. To get back on a winning streak, she hired Argentinean coach Carlos Rodriguez. He told her to go back and strike at the original source of her anger by expressing it to her previous coach, Yu Liqiao of the traditional Chinese system. Li Na followed his suggestion and told Coach Yu how her constant stream of criticism was scary and hurtful. She later commented: "After that, this burden was gone." Her play improved immediately.

Because Li Na has immense influence in China as a sports hero, she is inspiring them to embrace new levels of emotional expression, and Chinese youth appreciate her courage in saying no to the traditional system. After winning the Australian Open in 2014, Li Na retired because of knee injuries and is establishing a tennis academy in China.

Tracking Body Awareness

Last year, my husband ruptured a disk hiking the five-hundred-mile Colorado Trail up and over the Rocky Mountains. His physical recovery after surgery involved learning to receive his symptoms as feedback about what was good for his back and what wasn't. Rather than following his typical habit of pushing through discomfort, he listened and identified what motion or activity preceded the pain. Attention to his inner body awareness has helped him recover quickly and prevent further injury. Body sensations are an important part of our physical and emotional feedback system.

RIM sessions have revealed several effective ways to locate magnetic emotional forces. Tracking body awareness is one of them. It's an effective way to uncover harmful events stuck in memory. Rather than resisting the magnetic pull, we patiently let it attract our attention and take us to the charge. As RIM facilitators, we call this *neutral witnessing*. Whatever shows up is welcome and absent of any evaluation as good or bad, even when it seems evasive or defensive. We follow the imagery because we trust the emotional system. Following one's natural process establishes safety at an implicit level. Clients are incapable of doing it wrong because they are the expert of their own process.

When there's no one to resist and nothing to defend, our attention naturally goes where it's needed, similar to white blood cells automatically moving to an infection site. For example, Carol is with a "really good man," yet she notices she's sabotaging the relationship. When she closes her eyes and begins following her inner experience, there's red-hot energy in her midsection. Moving into it, she feels anger but doesn't want to explore it. After welcoming the feeling of "not wanting to explore it," we ask her imagination to reveal who is speaking, and a stubby, cartoonish guy named "Sam" shows up. He's stubborn and cynical. Carol is curious and dialogues with him to discover more. It becomes clear that he functions to slow her down so she doesn't get into trouble. Once he feels appreciated, he becomes friendly and helpful and joins Carol on her journey.

Carol responds to the question, "What are you experiencing now?" with awareness of pain in the back of her neck. Exploring the form of the pain, she moves into an amorphous, yellow, swirling energy. Inside the energy is an uncomfortable feeling of containment, and she calls in a virtual mentor for comfort. Accompanied by the character Sam and her mentor Archangel Michael, Carol is feeling ready to explore this containment. As she sits safely in it, the energy fades and becomes a mellow space.

Suddenly she remarks with anxiety: "There's a sharp claw digging into my spine. It really hurts, and I want to get rid of it." Bringing her companions Sam and Michael for safety, she goes to the point of the claw. When asked what's here, she senses her seven-year-old self when she learns that her best friend is being sexually abused. No one knows, and her friend asks Carol not to tell. Carol suffers for her friend and feels guilty she isn't doing anything to help. She's "caught between a rock and a hard spot."

Carol spontaneously gets in touch with a new feeling she's never realized before (implicit memory) of intense sexual curiosity regarding the abuse. The thought of it confuses her and makes her sick to her stomach, but there's curiosity. In this deep inner remembering, the connections fall into place, and Carol realizes how her unrecognized sexual exploring has shown up in her adult sexual acting out, including working as a stripper for a brief time. Suddenly it's all making sense, and she feels compassion for her younger self. Finding the compassion in her body, she senses it as a soft pink energy. She embraces it.

To the question "Would you like to redo your childhood experience with your best friend who's being abused?" Carol enthusiastically answers yes. Asking her imagination to take her (and her mentors) back to this original experience, Carol is given the opportunity to rewind time and speak to her friend: "I'm only seven years old. This secret is too painful to keep because you're my best friend and I love you—I can't stand to see you suffer." Her friend responds positively and together they share the secret with Carol's parents, who take charge of the problem. It is such a relief in Carol's young body, she feels light and free like an innocent girl.

After her session, Carol returns to her relationship with new feelings of innocence and self-compassion. She's more willing to be soft and share her vulnerable feelings, which creates greater closeness with her boyfriend.

Our human ego wants to keep us safe, but it operates at a visceral survival level that isn't concerned with insight from the higher brain—it's fighting for its life. We can shift out of this alarm mode as Carol did and access our more evolved self.

Asking for an Image of the One to Whom You Need to Speak

Another way to access a magnetic event is to ask your imagination for the answer. When you ask for an image of the one to whom you need to speak, you engage the creative brain. The idea of creative imagination was introduced by Carl Jung. He considered dream content to be a meaningful creative projection from the unconscious and actively worked with these images for better psychological outcomes.

In general, imagination has received little research attention, because we don't know how to quantify it. The Imagination Institute, however, in 2015 received a $5.6 million grant from the John Templeton Foundation and is funding studies that are "Advancing the Science of Imagination."

During my forty years of professional and personal experience, I've observed imagination to be astutely and consistently accurate and purposeful, similar to what Jung found. Early in the development of RIM, I worked with a woman hospitalized for the surgical removal of an aggressive malignant brain tumor. In her session prior to surgery, her virtual resource revealed that her condition was related to angry thoughts and was "like a strong wind that will quickly pass." As a nurse with knowledge of this kind of brain cancer, I thought she must be fooling herself, although I didn't say anything.

The doctors and I were all wrong, and her virtual mentor was right. During her craniotomy, they removed a bacterial abscess. After three weeks of IV antibiotics, she recovered completely. This event proved to me the immense credibility of one's imagination to interpret and identify body experience independent of medical diagnosis.

Magnetic images and the speed in which they appear can be quite astounding. As I start a phone session with an entertainer named Tara, she begins: "Okay, just give me a minute to get rid of this homeless man, then I can concentrate." After clarifying that he is in her mind and not a physical person, I say, "Whoa! Don't get rid of him. He's here for a reason."

When Tara engages with the homeless figure on the beach, she discovers that he represents a fear of financial insecurity if she pursues her dream of changing careers. As they converse, she moves into him and feels what his homelessness truly expresses:

he represents the part of her that wants to live completely free of responsibility. As she gives him a voice, her hidden desire becomes apparent.

She calls forth an image representing the career she is leaving, and a driven, frustrated musician shows up. When the two images dialogue, the conversation reveals that Tara needs some financial planning, which is not her strength—in fact, that is part of the responsibility she wants to avoid. However, the image of homelessness gets her attention in a way that a warning from her financial planner would not, and it works. Tara expends the time and energy to work out the details. She sells her house and in essence becomes "homeless," using the money to fund a new sustainable career.

Magnetizing New Empowering Memory

Once we find the highly charged root experience and defuse it, a regenerated image can integrate in memory. For example, Tara eventually sees the homeless man merge with her driven, career self. Her imagination manifests a new blended image of a caring, successful woman who is responsible and takes greater risks to try exciting things. She chooses to act in ways that keep her safe while allowing for greater adventure.

A way to magnetize the image of this successful and excited woman is to ingest it into the body, a process inspired by Dr. Gerald Jampolsky's guided imagery. Tara takes the new movie, folds it very small, and turns it into an edible form—maybe her favorite food or beverage. Then she imagines putting it in her mouth and swallowing it. As she senses her body digesting the image, the movie automatically multiplies itself into fifty trillion copies, and a movie lands on every one of her fifty trillion cells. She senses these movies playing on every cell from the top of her head to the tips of fingers and toes, from the center of her spine and out into every pore of her skin. She and her new image are one.

Repeatedly Lighting Up a New Habit

We know from research that the brain incorporates daily experiences into habit in about thirty days. Thus, reimagining your new positive images for a month causes your brain to light up and deepen new neurological pathways. As the brain's electricity is directed toward the new pathways, imprints of the past completely wither and shrink. They literally disintegrate and lose their ability to spark.

PRACTICE IT YOURSELF

Organically Uncovering Magnetic Memory Activities

In the following three-part activity, you will begin by tracking your body awareness, then ask your imagination to call up the image of the person you need to speak with to discharge a sabotaging/limiting magnetic charge. Finally, you will magnetize a new empowering memory. You can do this activity in your mind, or you can sense (with eyes open or closed) and write your experience on paper as you go. You can also work with a friend to guide each other. Begin by writing down a question or issue you'd like greater insight about.

Tracking Body Awareness

- With eyes open or closed, sense what is calling your attention in your body. Giving your attention to it completely; notice if it has a specific shape or is amorphous. Notice its size, form, color, temperature, texture, and density.

- Moving your attention into it, sense what's happening now.

- Continuously follow your spontaneous inner sensations and move into them for ten minutes or longer if needed.

Identify each sensation by completing the statement: "What I'm experiencing now is . . ."

- Finish the sentence: "What I've learned about the issue I identified in the beginning is . . ."

- At the end of this part of the process, sense through imagination: "What I've learned about myself through this experience so far is . . ."

Asking Imagination to Whom You Need to Speak

- Take some time to relax and focus on your breathing (feel free to use some soft music).

- Asking your soul to bring in the image of a perfect virtual resource, the details of who appears and where this resource is located easily materialize through your imagination.

- As you grow safe with this loving and powerful presence, ask your imagination to flash an image of the one to whom you need to speak. Receiving whoever pops up first, you let go of any desire to edit, even if what comes up doesn't make sense.

- Explore the details of this person with open curiosity, noticing appearance and location related to you.

- Write or speak aloud to this person directly and share in an uncensored, free-flowing way whatever comes into your mind. Begin with "What I want to say to you, (name of the person), that I've never said before is . . ."

- Your virtual resource is always with you, providing safety for both you and the person to whom you speak.

- Keep writing or speaking directly to this person as long as you sense feelings inside.

- Notice how it feels to share these feelings directly with this person by writing them down or speaking them aloud.

- Sense this person receiving what you've expressed like a stream of colored energy.

Magnetizing New Empowering Memory Activity

- Locate your virtual resource and again sense this presence around you.

- Your virtual resource shows you a new self-affirming movie of how you look and act differently now that you have expressed your feelings and discharged magnetized feelings. Take a minute to receive it.

- Noticing yourself in this new positive movie, sense the difference in your eyes and presence. Also notice how you move, talk, and decide differently.

- Take this new positive movie and fold it up very small, turning it into an edible form—maybe your favorite food or beverage.

- Imagine ingesting it in whatever way is appropriate to its form.

- As your body digests it, the new movie automatically multiplies into fifty trillion copies—and a movie lands on every one of the fifty trillion cells in your body. Sense them on every cell from the top of your head to the tips of your fingers and toes, from the center of your spine and out into every square inch of your body into every pore of your skin.

- Now sense this movie playing everywhere inside you.

- Notice how this feels and write it down.

You are born to fly
Through old memories into new life
Stickiness dissolves and confidence returns
You are all you ever wanted to be
Already and Always

SQUEEZE & BREEZE

Your Feelings Increase with Resistance and Decrease with Embrace

Sometimes it is harder to deprive oneself of a pain than of a pleasure. —F. Scott Fitzgerald, Tender Is the Night

The ideals which have lighted me on my way and time after time have given me new courage to face life cheerfully, have been Truth, Goodness, and Beauty. —Albert Einstein

Finding the beauty in your ugly feelings allows them to blossom and die away. Learn how this process happens organically in the following remarkable stories.

SUE'S STORY: WHAT THE BODY KNOWS

Sue Lewis from California and Chanda Carlson from the state of Washington are accountability partners in the RIM Facilitator Program. They meet weekly on the phone to practice. During one session, they discover Sue's body and virtual mentor have some very interesting information to reveal about the source of her physical pain.

Breathing through her forehead, down into her throat, heart, belly, and base of her spine, Sue gradually settles. Feeling relaxed, she spontaneously recalls California's Big Sur coast and delights in the ocean sounds, pine scents, and salty tastes. She feels water between her toes and mounds of burrowed sand crabs beneath her feet. Imagining crabbing with her dad, she feels warmth.

Sue becomes aware of numbness on the underside of her right arm; it has been there before. She feels scared as she remembers the horrible arm and neck pain she suffered last year. As she is guided into her throbbing armpit, a thought arrives: "You do too much . . . your right arm wants balance."

Sensing that her right arm wants to be heard, she is guided to speak aloud for it: "There is something amiss between us [both arms] that needs correcting."

The left arm responds: "I don't remember what, but there is something wrong. It feels defensive."

Sue senses the right arm responding to the left arm: "You're the one with the problem—I'm fine. You know what to do." Sue doesn't understand this and asks for clarification. The right arm responds: "There's something between us physically—a block—that needs to be cleared because the energy doesn't go back and forth."

She has no understanding of what's been shared, so she calls a virtual mentor to interpret. Jake, Sue's puppy, shows up and responds to both arms: "You two have been struggling for years—you're left-handed and everyone wanted you to be right-handed.

It's time to come together; it's not about everyone else! Come to terms and work together."

This is news to Sue; she has no conscious recall of this issue. However, it makes sense because she's dyslexic and has left-right confusion. Thirty-some years ago while she was working with reparenting therapists, they reported that she changes her hand dominance whenever she's in "the child" position. Sue still must consciously remember to flip her car turn signal; otherwise, she automatically turns on the windshield wipers. Similarly, she begins piano duets playing her part and unconsciously switches to her partner's part without realizing it, which frustrates the heck out of both players.

Sue receives what puppy Jack has expressed like a stream of colored energy; it looks like a rainbow coming into her midsection below her ribs. She speaks: "It makes perfect sense. I had no idea. I'll bet after this my piano playing improves."

As facilitator Chanda guides Sue to clap her hands together to blend what's been voiced by both arms, the yellow and white word "PEACE" pops into her cupped hands, and Sue comments how the aggravation she's felt for a long time is significantly reduced.

Checking in with her body, she finds a nagging dot of red-hot energy. When asked what she wants to do with it, Sue says: "Throw it out and stomp on it." Using her imagination, she lifts out the small red spot and stomps it until it disappears. Scanning her body, Sue notices a feeling of completion with the unwanted images gone.

After this session, Sue realizes that her right/left confusion with the turn signal has disappeared and the numbness she used to feel when playing the piano is absent. She has a massage and enjoys what was impossible before:

I had a massage and much to my amazement my body was completely open to it. I know this sounds strange but I had no idea it was possible to feel so good and pain-free. Somehow my body is more open to receiving the benefits. Also I'm more aware when I'm tensing my shoulders in some kind of anticipation of something unpleasant about to happen—this is a long-standing habit carried over from childhood. My upper body tends to be tense. Now I am reminded automatically to relax my shoulders. What a wonderful realization!

Sue's story shows how pain can be a directive from the body about what's wrong. When she moves into the throbbing in her armpit, she uncovers a conflict that occurred when she was born left-handed and was pushed to be right-handed. Her left-right confusion disappears after her arms come to an understanding. The body knows things the mind doesn't.

MIRIAM AND WILL'S STORY: GUILT CONSTRICTS THOSE WE LOVE

Miriam attends a group workshop and brings her twenty-three-year-old son. She's hoping he'll get assistance with his financial struggles. When Miriam introduces herself, to her surprise she begins to cry. She doesn't understand, so she's guided to close her eyes and sense what's in the tears, where she discovers that although her current life is financially abundant, a past choice is haunting her: "I feel so guilty about the poor decisions I made that created a financially deprived childhood for my son Will." She senses the size, shape, and color of this sadness in her body, drops into it, and speaks directly to her son from it: "Will, I'm so sorry. I hate it that I was such a foolish single mom to bring you into my financially insecure world. I wish with all my heart I could have done it differently."

Will accurately mirrors what his mom says and then responds:

Mom, I feel good about my childhood. From my perspective, we were normal, and I was loved. I feel I've had a great upbringing.

> It's important for me that you believe this, because if you hold on to this guilt, it suggests there's something wrong with me, and that doesn't feel good or true.

Miriam receives his words, mirrors them, and responds: "Will, I love you more than anything, and I don't want to do anything that makes you feel bad. The guilt is not about you; it's about me. And I hear you saying my guilt suggests something's lacking in you and you want me to let it go and trust that you are fine." She laughs: "Okay, I get it." Miriam looks for the guilt in her body, and surprisingly it's gone.

Mother and son embrace in a forgiving and loving hug as the group wipes away their own tears. Miriam and Will arrive at a new understanding that brings them closer and supports greater success for both. They show how holding on to guilt can negatively influence those we love.

NATHAN'S STORY: GAINING INSIGHT THROUGH ANOTHER'S EYES

Nathan is an extremely successful San Francisco physician who engages in a RIM journey to improve his declining relationships with four siblings. Originally from India, he's an adept meditator and begins his journey with a lovely display of color and light. His sensory experience spontaneously leads him to an image of his younger brother, who died when he was little, and deeply buried grief explodes. In this safe space, the two brothers experience a profound emotional reunion, and Nathan's heart opens instantly. They share unexpressed sadness and love, and the pain of separation fades.

Nathan asks this brother to help him with their other brothers, and he agrees.

An image of the siblings sitting in a half circle arises, and Nathan speaks to them all. Because they are significantly less successful than he is, he suggests how they could excel. When he shifts to look from their eyes, he senses the superiority he's communicated and recognizes with sad surprise: "I'm diminishing their souls." It's an eye-opening moment because he thought he was helping them. He writes a few months later: "You won't be surprised to learn my relationship with all of my brothers is transformed. I'm so grateful." Nathan's story teaches how viewing our behavior through another's eyes uncovers what's not working. The minute Nathan saw the pain he was causing and changed, his relationships changed too!

HOW IT WORKS—PRACTICALLY AND SCIENTIFICALLY

It is a common human desire to want to be happy. We don't want to feel angry, guilty, shameful, or envious. We frequently try to remove these undesirable emotions and hope they won't return. Although they can be consciously forgotten, what we try to avoid and deny is only suppressed in the subconscious and becomes harder to release—just like ugly fabric stains.

We can learn to wash away unwanted feelings by metaphorically understanding the physical action of soap and water to remove persistent stains. The cleaning action for fabric stains is found in tiny spheres called micelles. These little guys are coated on the outside with water-loving groups that encase a fat-loving pocket, which surrounds grease particles and causes them to disperse and fall away.

Normally oil and water do not mix, but soap "loves" the water and "loves" the grease particle it surrounds, allowing them to come together and disperse gently. We have learned through the real-life stories in this chapter that when we move toward rejected emotions and surround them with loving attention, they quickly break into manageable bits until they are gone. Once our inner resistance is dissolved, we return to a beautifully open and receptive state of mind where our dreams can manifest naturally.

Beauty in the Ugliness

You're at an elegant dinner in your finest clothes having a wonderful time—and it happens. You're talking and eating and a dribble hits the bull's-eye on your dress or tie for all to see. Oh, the embarrassment! We've all felt it. It happened to me the night of my senior prom when I learned marinara sauce does not wash easily out of pink chiffon. All night, my attention was self-consciously stuck on that ugly spot and what others must be thinking about it. I felt less than elegant.

Such is the case with ugly feelings. Something happens and you automatically feel less than pleasing. Those "damned" feelings like anger, sadness, and envy we talked about in chapter one are back, and you hate feeling them. Now you are managing both the hated feeling plus the self-hate for feeling it. Have I mentioned the fear that others may see your hatefulness?

The word *ugly* originated in 1200–1250 from Middle English *ugly, uglike* from the Old Norse *uggligr,* meaning "fearful or dreadful."[1] Synonyms include "disagreeable, unpleasant, mean, and quarrelsome," suggesting ugly feelings arise when we don't like how things are going. What we like and don't like is personal; what's unpleasant for one person may be no big deal for another.

Antonyms of ugly include "beautiful, pleasing, agreeable."[2] Most of us long to have beautiful lives. Yet, beauty is a moving target. There's an Ugly Models Agency in London where they value faces with character instead of "bland perfection" and have clients like Diesel and Calvin Klein. Beauty and ugliness are not opposites; rather they are aspects of the same thing, suggests author Stephen Bayley.[3] For example, today we consider mountains beautiful—while there was a time they were considered dangerous, frightening, and home to nasty demons and bandits.

The same is true with emotions. Ugly and beautiful feelings are aspects of the same normal system. Unpleasant feelings are equally as natural to life as the heavenly ones. Though uncomfortable, they benefit us and our relationships. We grow from engaging with them. When we embrace and understand our ugly feelings, we gain greater self-awareness, choice, and a return to inherent joy.

We've all experienced stubborn emotional stains—a feeling that holds over from an undesirable experience or the lack of a desirable one. To carry on the metaphor of how soap removes stains, the logical question is: "What works as soap to wash ugly feelings?" It is self-compassion and self-love. When we find compassion for ourselves and others, emotional stains soften and gently fade. No longer a testimonial to our humiliating defects, they become a testament to our humanity, which connects us with every human on the planet. We're not alone.

Russ demonstrates how his organic emotional system naturally cleans emotional stains when he patiently embraces them. He's an attractive man in his early forties who has never married. Then he meets a woman he really likes and lives with her on the East Coast. Russ wants this relationship to work, but he remembers the upheaval and hurt he experienced after his parents' divorce, and he's frightened and self-conscious.

Closing his eyes, he begins a compelling, focused journey through his body. First, he senses an energy in his right kidney; it's the shape of a potato with a navy/gray smooth, dry surface. It's hollow and surrounded by misty fog. As he moves into it, he gets a sensation of pain that rises into his face. As he follows these sensations, there come a warmth through his chest and a lessening of tension in his body. Red energy moves up his throat then down. As he rides it, he gets an image of the family home where he grew up. There are lights in the windows making it look welcoming, but when he enters, it's dark inside, stirring his anxiety. When he finds the switch and turns on the lights, he feels better. Standing in this familiar house, he gets a weird feeling in his lower belly that's "slimy, yellow and gray, without much vitality and not healthy."

He calls for a virtual resource, and Arielle, an angel, shows up. It feels good to have her accompany him into the ugly energy, where he feels compelled by a river of small, red eggs floating from his gut. "These are my original memories of home, and they are vanishing." As he flows with them, it's like moving in a molten lava flow, and he notices greater energy and aliveness in the bottom half of his body. Arielle says to him: "*This too shall pass, Russ. There's nothing to worry about. Feel your legs.*" A white light blankets the sliminess and dissolves it. Yellow bubbles carry away the pressure, and "Mother Nature absorbs them."

A sliver of black to the left on his back catches his attention. As he enters it, an image of a four-year-old Russ pops up. He's playing at the family's country cabin. As the adult Russ looks into the boy's eyes, he finds "innocence, clarity, and purity, and on his shoulders is warm, golden light."

Russ and the angel Arielle hold the four-year-old and experience "buoyancy and fun and life seems less serious." A spacious, bright, blue-and-white sky calls Russ's attention, and he moves into it. Here there is great relaxation and a feeling of "infinite possibility, optimism, hope, and ease without effort." He feels himself sinking into something to the left—it's cool milk that changes into a swirling ball of light that moves through his body and out his right shoulder. He senses that it is "cleaning me out." There's tingling around his eyebrows and forehead with golden light. His head grows to double its size like a seedpod floating in blackness, and the boy suddenly feels scared and alone. He asks the adult Russ and Arielle to come together, and they do: "We're a team. Life's better, more fun and joyful and lighthearted. Thank you for coming back." Golden, warm energy streams between the threesome into Russ's belly.

When we ask Arielle for a video of how Russ looks and acts differently over the two weeks following this inner work, her images reveal him with more "swagger, decisiveness, fun, and clarity." There's "less clutter" in his mind, and he sees himself playing full out in this new relationship and career change. He remarks afterwards: "That old pain of watching my parents suffer had to clear out in order for me to have something different. I feel so much lighter and more optimistic that I can be in a relationship and be happy; it's a new feeling and I like it."

A year later, I run into Russ again. He's confident and playful. His relationship is going well, and he's planning a marriage proposal. By embracing the reality of his parents' painful divorce, Russ's body and soul took him on a self-generated journey of organic release. Each molecule of his being was sensed in graphic and sensory ways as the residue dissolved.

Expanded Self-Awareness

The human ego doesn't like looking stupid, vulnerable, or bad. Yet when you allow yourself to embrace ugly feelings, you invite greater self-awareness. By saying yes to these feelings, a door opens to reveal self-sabotaging patterns, distorted feelings, and misjudged beliefs. As best-selling author Iyanla Vanzant says: "The truth will set you free, but you have to endure the labor pains of birthing it." The good news is you are learning how to accelerate this birth and minimize the pain.

The more curious you are about your ugly feelings, the faster you grow and excel. People in the stories you've read demonstrate a willingness to dive into their feelings, rather than merely talking about them from an intellectual perspective. Embracing our ugliness is a courageous act in defiance of the critical ego, which seeks to keep us safe through rationalizations and emotional distance. When we welcome painful feelings instead, we receive immediate relief, effective action plans, and the confidence to execute them.

When Patty engages in a group RIM, she's totally frustrated because the childhood images in her imagination keep replaying her vivid anger with her dad that has carried on throughout her life. But when her imagination is asked to bring up an image of the person to whom she needs to speak, it's not her dad but rather her mom. Patty is furious and resists because her mom has been her biggest cheerleader and they have always been good friends. Leaving the group frustrated, she tells her roommate how the group RIM didn't work because it "couldn't be her mom."

She wakes the next morning and becomes immersed in drying her hair when an inner voice breaks in to say: *"Of course it's your mom, stupid!"* Revelations come barreling in: she's spent her life being angry with her dad when actually she is angry with her mom for not standing up to her dad and protecting her and her sisters from him. She spends thirty minutes crying and later shares: "It was like this huge stone I had been dragging around for years lifted off of me; it left me empty—a good empty—so I could fill it up with my soul and be with all the good things life has to offer. I feel calm and peace."

Discovering Our "Ugliness" through Another's Perspective

As mentioned in chapter three, empathy is essential to good relationships. When we are able to appreciate another's actual experience, we don't rely on our distorted projection of their motives; we go directly to the source without confusing the situation with our own fears and defensiveness. As you've witnessed in numerous real-life stories, when we actually imagine looking from another's eyes, we begin to appreciate their feelings and insights that are independent of us. We gain compassion for their vulnerability and receive new information about what isn't working and how we could be different in the relationship. This information is critical to acting in new ways as you saw in Miriam's interaction, where it became clear that her guilt about how she raised her son implied he was damaged. Similarly, Nathan's interaction with his siblings actually diminished them. It gets simple when we move out of our egocentric rationalizations and allow ourselves to receive others' feelings.

When you look at yourself through another's perspective, you gain insights not normally available. When my son was interviewing for a summer job during high school, it wasn't going well. To get a sense of what wasn't working, I suggested he close his eyes and imagine looking from the perspective of the job interviewer. Shocked, he saw himself as a timid, hesitant teen. He didn't feel insecure, but his body reflected his inexperience. Once he saw the specific problem, he could correct it. Now he could speak with confidence instead. When he could close his eyes and see himself this way, he knew he was ready. The result: he earned a very responsible job that paid more than he expected and looked great on his résumé.

Another benefit of seeing how we look through another's perspective is that it allows us to locate and rewire an original problematic event and gain healing and behavioral change; it happens in the body at the site where the emotion is stored. Justin is a successful organizational consultant with twin sons in high school. When he became a single dad, effective parenting was important to him. He had grown up in a traditional family with an extremely domineering father. When Justin looks from his sons' perspective, he sees the same paternal behaviors he hated in his own upbringing.

As Justin goes back in time and speaks to his father, he releases a mountain of smoldering rage. As he bridges a new emotional connection with his dad, he realizes it's never too late. Using his regenerated father-son connection as a model, he enacts a close, playful relationship with his sons that grows more enjoyable through their high school and college years.

When we're willing to embrace our ugliness, we transform. Many people automatically look and behave differently after doing this depth of inner work. Going beneath talk to direct experience, we immediately record new images in emotional memory, resulting in different spontaneous behaviors. A middle-aged anesthesiologist uncovered hidden sorrow held over from third grade, when she had returned to school from a prolonged illness and found her best friend had replaced her. Looking at this experience through her friend's eyes, she discovered she never shared her hurt feelings (a pattern in her marriage, too). After acknowledging her feelings aloud to herself and her friend during RIM, she got a different outcome emotionally and physically. She commented a few weeks later:

> I had a strange experience. I've been going to yoga class with my best friend for six years. I never talk during class except to her. At the end of this week's class, I realized I'd initiated three spontaneous conversations with other women. It was so much fun, and I wasn't even thinking about it.

When the source experience is rewired, we see everything differently. A journalist who had experienced RIM asked: "What's the difference between therapy and RIM?" I deflected to him: "You've experienced both. What do you think is different?" He paused thoughtfully and replied: "When I leave a therapy session, I feel good. Going through RIM—this deep, body experience—I feel physically different." He's not the first person to say, "I feel like a different person." The magic of organically clearing human self-consciousness allows a quick return to childlike joy and curiosity, which naturally express as a sparkle in the eyes.

Realizing New Choices

When we look deep within and recognize hidden feelings and their effects, a new world of possibility opens. We can make insightful choices rather than emotionally driven ones.

Lucy is an older mom with a grade school daughter. After they clash in intense power struggles, Lucy is depressed and immobilized. She loves her daughter so much she'd do anything for her, but it doesn't help. Lucy can't see any effective options. She's driven to be unconditionally loving till she can't take it anymore and becomes angry and disapproving—neither extreme works. When she tunes in to her body, she discovers she's stuck in the fear of being an "inadequate" mother and "mean" person.

Her imagination spontaneously recalls a comical image of her favorite uncle entertaining her by suspending a pea just above his lips with his breath. Her childlike joy and curiosity are resurrected as seriousness dissolves. It's as if the spell of her previous obsessiveness has been broken, and she feels light and free as she views the clash between herself and her daughter. Instantly she recognizes another choice. She can set limits with her daughter in a lighter, playful, and matter-of-fact way.

Looking from her daughter's perspective, Lucy senses how the previous parental seriousness felt judging, while this neutral limit-setting feels like *"It's what mom's do"*—it's her job. She's not a bad mom and her daughter isn't a bad kid, rather everyone's in the process of learning. When Lucy makes this new choice, she grows into an effective mom, and her daughter grows into a normal grade-schooler.

Numerous people have discovered through RIM journeys that a chronic health symptom/illness is highlighting their choices. Rosie is extremely distressed after being diagnosed with type 2 diabetes. When she asks her imagination for an image to represent the diabetes, a huge spider named Harry appears. Harry's gargantuan size and fierce appearance cause Rosie to shrink in her chair. Harry speaks: "I'm here to help you take better care of your body. If you take care of yourself, you'll live a normal, long life." As he speaks, he shrinks to normal size and seems more "friendly." Rosie is a nurse, so she knows he's right and says to him: "Harry, I feel you are my friend and you're helping me live a healthier life. Thank you. Let's communicate directly each day when I first wake up and go to bed, so I know how I'm doing. I know you'll be honest with me so I can't fool myself." Rosie demonstrates how life experiences that initially appear scary and ugly can turn out to be a friendly support that helps us take better care of ourselves.

Ask your imagination to call forth a number between one and ten, with ten being most as to your level of self-awareness. Circle the number below.

1	2	3	4	5	6	7	8	9	10

You'll be able to play with your level of self-awareness in the Practice It Yourself section of this chapter.

A Return to Inherent Joy

Babies and children return naturally to their organic state of joy and curiosity after pain dissolves. Todd is a seven-year-old who can't sleep for fear of monsters in the closet. The problem begins after he's in a golf cart accident with his grandfather. They are riding for fun and accidentally flip the cart. Fortunately, nothing gets injured, except Todd's feeling of safety. He can't sleep and is constantly anxious.

Todd chooses to have his mom sit quietly next to him as he closes his eyes, although many children don't during their RIM sessions. As is common in young people, his vivid imagination takes off, and I'm holding on trying to keep up. He senses an image of the golf cart and feels immediate fear. Around the cart are numerous moving vehicles—airplanes, cars, etc.—and he's overwhelmed: "They are everywhere. It's not safe."

When he calls in a virtual mentor, the sun speaks to him: "Todd, I'm here for you and I power the earth." At this moment, Todd sees the sun send out bolts of electricity that move the vehicles, and he's reassured. Speaking to the golf cart, he says: "How could you do that? My granddad and I didn't do anything to you. You could have hurt us. I'm mad at you. You scared me, and now I'm scared of every big thing that moves."

Todd senses the cart's response: "Todd, I didn't mean for that to happen. I have a very heavy body, it gained momentum as it rolled down that steep hill, and I couldn't hold it back. I'm sorry. Will you forgive me? I like you and I want to be your friend."

Todd receives what the cart has expressed like a stream of colored energy, and as his body fills with rainbow light, he responds: "Okay, I'll be your friend, but don't do that again. It's nice to know you didn't mean to hurt us. Will you let me safely ride you by myself for fun?"

"Yes," says the cart, who wears a friendly smile as he rolls close to Todd. They have a great time playing together and riding wherever Todd wants to go—always with the powerful sun shining safety down on them. They make friends with all the vehicles, who have also acquired friendly smiles.

The sun then lifts Todd from the cart and carries him to the bottom of the ocean, where there's a huge clam with a pearl. Todd breathes effortlessly and asks: "What am I doing here?"

The clam answers: "Todd, you are here because you're a very special boy who knows a lot about life. You are here to share your wisdom, and this pearl is a gift for you." Todd puts the pearl in his pocket and is magically transported back to the chair in my office, where he says: "I've confronted my fears and received the pearl of wisdom. I'm done." Then he opens his eyes—his fears and anxiety are also done.

You have the same childlike ability to regain faith in life immediately. When you embrace your ugly feelings and survive, your heart develops trust in your emotional resilience, and it opens to feel greater joy. This is your birthright; you've just needed to learn how it works.

After Todd's journey, his mom shares that he's happier than he's been since they moved to Denver a year earlier. After the session, he asks classmates over to play and develops close friends. Todd's journey is his own, not a prescribed process. He went where he needed to go, and I followed in amazement. He showed how easy it really is when we remember the childlike curiosity and magical aspects of our nature. Todd's journey also provided an example of how special gifts may be revealed spontaneously when we visit these deep inner spaces.

Embracing ugly feelings causes them to die away to reveal natural states of peace and love. Some people even find their way to great revelations. Josh is a twenty-eight-year-old Israeli man who does a Skype session because he is feeling called to inspire others through speaking rather than through his paintings, which have provided his livelihood up to this point. As he follows his body sensations, he finds an energetic block in his chest and throat. He moves into it, and senses an experience he had at four years old when his mom becomes very irritated with him for bringing yogurt instead of butter to the dinner table. The sensitive little boy feels very hurt when shamed for this innocent mistake and speaks to her about his feelings.

As he moves to look out of his mom's eyes, he senses great insecurity in her body. When he asks for an image of the source of it, scenes from the Holocaust come rushing in. His virtual mentor Jesus lifts him to view the Holocaust from above. The graphic scenes are horrific, and Josh sobs and writhes in emotional pain. With Jesus supporting him, he grieves this historic loss of innocence. The feelings flow intensely until he eventually reaches a place of emptiness where there is communication without words from Jesus, and Josh accepts that it happened yet can't be explained. As the grief completes its course, his awareness reminds him of a recent incident when Israelis burned a live baby. He feels intense sadness for the Palestinians and especially the parents of this baby. After the session ends, he makes a video apology to the Palestinians in Arabic on YouTube and acknowledges that there is no excuse for Israelis to kill in this way, regardless of what others have done to them. He feels changed and ready to continue stepping into his new career goal.

A rose is a great metaphor for the nature of emotion. The aesthetic beauty of the blossom with its velvety texture and sweet scent can be appreciated only at the risk of braving the thorns. Gardeners consider the thorn a practical protection from animals and humans, and the Greeks have a proverb to express their integral relationship: "From a thorn comes a rose, and from a rose comes a thorn." Abraham Lincoln insightfully suggested: "We can complain because rose bushes have thorns, or rejoice because thorn bushes have roses." Similarly, we can complain because life has ugly feelings, or we can appreciate them as catalysts to greater love and compassion.

PRACTICE IT YOURSELF

Expanding Self-Awareness Activity

- Ask your imagination to flash in your mind a number between one and ten of your level of self-awareness, with ten being most. Circle it below:

....

1   2   3   4   5   6   7   8   9   10

....

- As you step into whatever number that's been revealed, close your eyes and imagine how it feels to live in this level of self-awareness with hyperawareness of your feelings and results.

- Looking from this current perspective over to a "ten" level of maximum self-awareness, witness an image of how you would look, talk, act, and decide in a more self-aware way. Take a minute.

- Stepping into the "ten," look out of highly self-aware eyes at the world and notice how it feels.

- Looking through these more self-aware eyes at your future, ask your imagination to reveal how this difference gets better results. Take a minute.

- When you are ready, record or share your experience, noticing how you feel.

Identifying and Finding Beauty in Ugly Feelings Activity

- Take some time to get quiet, then imagine breathing through your heart.

- As your attention is in your heart, hear a word of what ugly feeling is ready to be cleared from your body right now.

- Sense where the energy of this feeling is resting in your body.

- Your imagination gives size, shape, and color to this energy. Notice the specifics.

- Call in at least one virtual resource to be with you until you feel safe.

- With your virtual resource accompanying you, move your attention into this energy and be in it as best as you can.

- As you sense this energy, express (speak/write) what you find using these sentence leads:

  - What feels ugly here is . . .
  - What I really hate is . . .
  - What's the most awful about it is . . .
  - Whatever else wants to be voiced, go ahead and freely speak/write . . .
  - What it's like to express all of this is . . .

- Express whatever is present, letting go of any desire to edit. Write/speak until you feel empty.

- Notice how the energy lightens as you easily allow it.

- Your heart brings up one word of how you feel now, and you receive it.

- Allowing this feeling as much as possible, find it in your body.

- Noticing its color and texture, move into this energy and rest in it as long as you want.

- When you are done, write or speak of your experience, noticing how you feel.

Seeing Yourself through Another's Perspective Activity

- Find a quiet, private space and settle into it.

- Closing your eyes, take whatever time you need to relax as your attention settles into your belly and senses the inside of your body like a 3-D movie.

- Imagine breathing in through your navel and out through the small of your back for several minutes until you feel very relaxed. Soft music without lyrics may be helpful.

- Imagine a magical screen in front of you, where your imagination flashes a picture or name of a person whom you need to hear from. Receive whoever shows up, letting go of any urge to edit.

- As you receive this image, notice who it is and how this person looks. Notice how you feel as you see this person.

- Moving your attention into this person, look out of his/her eyes. Through these eyes, look over at yourself and sense how you appear. Continuing to gaze from this other's perspective, sense this person's inner feelings and thoughts about you and relationship with you. Using these sentence leads, speak further for this person:

- What I haven't told you that you need to know (your name) is . . .

- What I've been hiding is . . . because . . .

- What I need from you is . . . because . . .

- What I love most about you is . . .

- My wish for our relationship is . . .

- What else wants to be spoken is . . .

- How it feels to speak this to you is . . .

- Returning your attention to yourself, look out of your own eyes at the person and notice how this person appears different now. Notice how you feel after sensing this person's inner feelings. If you want, speak/write to this person. Go ahead and express whatever else wants to be voiced, beginning with "As I hear you, I feel . . ." In the RIM process, you always get the last word.

- Take some time to record or verbally share your experience. New thoughts and awarenesses continue to arise as you write and speak about it.

Returning to Joy Activity

- Focusing on your breathing, imagine that air is flowing into the crown of your head, through your body, and out the palms of your hands and soles of your feet, and you become very relaxed.

- Asking your imagination for an image of you as a joyful baby or child, you easily receive it.

- Bringing in a virtual resource to be there with the little you, allow your attention to move into the center of this joyful baby/child.

- Relax into being this innocent soul, as your specific virtual resource makes sure you are safe and loved.

- Notice how it feels, and enjoy it in detail.

- Indulging yourself with full sensory experiences of what feels good, ask your virtual resource for everything you want and fully receive it.

- Notice how this feels.

- Find in your little body the energy of childlike joy.

- Sensing its color and texture, move into it and immerse yourself in it.

- Becoming one with this colored energy, you feel childlike joy as best you can.

- When your eyes open, record or share your experiences.

- Notice how you feel.

> *Feelings are the foundation of your mood*
> *Which is the attitude of your days,*
> *Which inspires a way of life*
> *Which generates feelings*
> *And so it goes . . .*

REDO & RENEW

What Is Real and What Is Imagined Reconsolidate as Your Emotional Memory

Be not the slave of your own past. Plunge into the sublime seas, dive deep and swim far, so you shall come back with self-respect, with new power, with an advanced experience that shall explain and overlook the old.

—RALPH WALDO EMERSON

I like nonsense, it wakes up the brain cells. Fantasy is a necessary ingredient in living, it's a way of looking at life through the wrong end of a telescope. Which is what I do, and that enables you to laugh at life's realities. —DR. SEUSS

Did you know your old memories can reconsolidate in new beneficial ways? When you do so, you rock your body and mood with good vibrations. Mike, Carla, and Donna have done it, and their stories demonstrate the process.

MIKE'S STORY: TRANSFORMATION IS TIMELESS

Mike is short, lean, and thirty-something. He's a physician with an excellent job, but he's unhappy. As he speaks, he seems unsure about his work, his relationship, his living situation, and just about everything. His contained demeanor and insecurity seem incongruent with his accomplishments.

As he moves his attention into his body, he notices a red swirling in his head. As he moves with the swirling, it calms, and he rests until his attention is drawn toward his gut where there's a blue heaviness. It's a deep, dark pool, and he dives into the bottom of it, where he asks for a number. "Six" pops into his mind with an image of six-year-old Mike. The adult Mike immediately recognizes the past event.

Mike is living with his aunt and cousin on a different island from his parents, so he can attend a better school. Mike's cousin Tom is the same age, and they go to school together. Mike remembers the horror of that time. His aunt is jealous of his mom and goes out of her way to demean Mike. Mike is given a bed in a closet, while his cousin's room is large with two beds. Tom bullies Mike constantly, and his mom always takes his side or looks the other way. Mike is furious but learns protesting will get him even greater punishment, so he becomes more and more passive while his cousin grows more aggressive.

Mike lives under these conditions for three years without saying anything to his parents because, being a good son, he feels they believe attending this school will improve his life. One summer his mom says: "Mike, what's wrong. You're not the same bright-eyed boy. You don't play or laugh anymore. I'm worried." When Mike shares the conditions at his aunt's, his parents immediately make different arrangements for his schooling.

Asking young Mike whom he needs to speak to, it's his cousin Tom at a time when he's acting especially mean. When he calls up a virtual resource, it is adult Mike who shows up to support the boy. Young Mike stands up to the bully: "You think you are so big because your mom lets you dominate me, but I'm done backing away from you. I want the toy you took from me; it's mine." With the support of his virtual resource, Mike tackles Tom and physically takes it back, saying: "I'm so mad at you for being mean and unfair. You didn't give me a chance, which is too bad. We could have fun together, but you've make that impossible. I'm done taking your bullying."

Mike walks away, and it feels so good to act on his own behalf. He finally feels a sense of justice and power. This feeling is a strong core through his boy body. He moves into it, and the strength expands into every cell, atom, and molecule.

When asked if he'd like to redo the whole experience, Mike enthusiastically agrees. The complete boyhood memory rewinds and pauses at the perfect moment for the regeneration of a new version: the first holiday phone call after Mike is at his aunt's. The new memory shows Mike telling his mother how awfully he is being treated by his cousin and aunt. She responds immediately by bringing him home. As he sails away, he sees his aunt and Tom are crestfallen because they have lost their power over him. He feels safe.

Mike is unstoppable. Rewinding the new memory once more, he jumps into it and imagines living it seven times. Each time more details show up, and the whole experience feels more and more alive in his body memory.

After this experience, Mike looks transformed—as if a fog has lifted from his presence. Others notice these changes and comment about the new sparkle in his eye. Some think he looks taller. He comments that he feels more confidence in himself than he's ever felt. Mike shows how it's never too late to have a happy childhood. Each of us has the personal power to transform our felt body experience anytime we choose.

CARLA'S STORY: REGENERATING A SILENCED VOICE

It's not uncommon for children who witness the abuse of siblings to suffer trauma. For no obvious reason, Carla's big sister Sherry is the object of her father's rages. When her sister is emotionally and physically abused, Carla cowers in fear and abject sadness. She hates her dad and hates herself even more because she is helpless to protect Sherry.

It is no surprise that Carla's older sister grows up overweight with severe medical problems. (Kaiser research shows adults with childhood trauma are more likely to have medical problems as adults.[1]) Without a successful career, she barely gets by, and Carla helps her financially. She is determined to help her sister become emotionally and physically healthy and to assist other abused women to thrive. Much to her dismay, Carla notices that she self-sabotages when she gets beyond a comfortable level of success.

Carla, who regularly meditates, finds it easy to settle into a relaxed, beautiful space where she senses a loving Buddha during her RIM journey. As she turns her attention to her body and brings in Buddha, she settles deeper into this image. Without external distractions, she notices something jittery in the pit of her stomach. It's like watching static on a screen and makes her feel nauseated. With Buddha by her side, she moves into the static. As she becomes one with the static, she asks for a number and "seven" comes to mind. When prompted, Carla's imagination brings an image of her seven-year-old self, and she gasps in terror—it's little Carla crouching against the wall, unable to breathe, as her sister is being hit by their father.

Swiftly and with a firm voice, we ask the Buddha to step between Dad and Sherry and create a force field of safety that Dad cannot penetrate. Meanwhile, Carla stands next to her sister and comforts her. Standing together, the sisters face a restrained Dad, and Carla speaks assertively for herself and Sherry:

> Daddy, you are mean. How can you do this to your own daughter? It's terrible, and I won't let you. I hate you. I hate you, and I hate it when you hit Sherry. She's at your mercy, as am I . . . until NOW. Now Buddha is more powerful than you, and you are stopped in your tracks. It feels so good to stop you with a power for good. Finally, I feel safe because I have done something to protect my sister. Thank you, Buddha.

Carla locates this new feeling of safety in her seven-year-old body just beneath her sternum. It's a big ball of fiery yellow and orange energy. Moving into it, soaking it up, and being it, Carla feels energized and confident. Looking from little Carla's eyes at the adult Carla, she says:

> Carla, see what I've done. I know you can be successful in creating women's empowerment programs. You were born to do this and now I feel safe, so I can help you. I'm so happy we are both here—together we are strong. We will speak our voice—no more hiding.

Carla facilitates several successful women's workshops over the next few months. The antiquated memory of her sister's abuse is changed to one of personal empowerment. Though the factual memory remains, Carla feels brave enough to interrupt abuse. In fact, I witness her confronting an aggressive male who verbally attacks a female speaker at a conference of a hundred people. Carla's reaction is automatic, quick, and strong. Afterward, many women in the audience thank her for her powerful response. They tell her how grateful they are that she stood up for them. Her new power is neurologically rocking her memory in a positive way. This story shows how important it is to express your voice. Furthermore, it's never too late to bring your voice to times in the past when you were silenced.

DONNA'S STORY: REGENERATING A PIVOTAL MOMENT ELEVATES SELF-ESTEEM

In her late twenties, Donna is getting worried she'll never marry. Dating hasn't come easy, and she no longer has the constant access to eligible men like at college. Although her career is progressing fabulously, Donna would like a husband and children and is becoming extremely impatient. In fact, she is beginning to feel hopeless because she has no idea how to change her single status.

As Donna closes her eyes, her awareness easily settles inside her body and she senses it as three-dimensional. Scanning her body for what is calling her attention, she senses a bloated feeling in her stomach. As we explore the size, shape, and color of this bloated feeling, it gradually becomes visible; it is a big, "yucky" amorphous blob occupying most of her stomach. The color is dark, almost black, and the texture is gooey. Its most compelling quality is this texture, which makes it seem heavy.

As Donna moves her attention into the gooiest part, she asks her imagination to bring up a spontaneous image representing the source. Right there, in a surprising flash, is the image of eleven-year-old Donna standing in the fifth-grade cafeteria line. Absent any awareness of why this scene has shown up, she starts searching for clues. Eventually, a classmate named Bobby appears. He points a finger at her and says abruptly: "You're ugly." Standing there in humiliated shock, Donna wants desperately to crawl under a table and hide. Instead, tears stream down the inside of her throat as she chokes them back.

Here it is—the exact moment of rejection that has been unconsciously punching Donna's self-image for fourteen years. Still, she hasn't consciously remembered it until now. It has hung out insidiously in the shadows of her mind, making her feel unattractive around men. Acting quickly to boost the unsuspecting eleven-year-old Donna, we ask her imagination to call in an image of a powerful and loving mentor, whereby her mother steps into the scene to her right and Donna instantly feels comfort and safety. With the support of her mother, Donna bravely speaks up to Bobby: "That hurts my feelings, Bobby. How can you be so mean?"

Shifting to look from Bobby's eyes, Donna is surprised to sense his response: "I didn't mean to hurt you. I just wanted your attention because I like you. That's how I interact with the guys, so I thought it would work with you too. I'm sorry."

As Donna receives Bobby's words and sentiments, she is relieved beyond belief. Never in her wildest dreams did she consider that he liked her! For the first time since fifth grade, without having to talk herself into it, she entertains the thought that she is attractive. As she stands to walk out the door, she radiates a new beauty with her head held high and a graceful feminine walk.

Within a few months of this session, Donna begins to date someone special. A year later, they are engaged. Today they are married with two beautiful children. Her story shows how imagination reveals essential insights never considered.

HOW IT WORKS—PRACTICALLY AND SCIENTIFICALLY

Since the onset of recorded history, people have remembered the same event differently. This self-generated perspective shows up in how we recall many past occurrences. Memory scientists find that our immediate descriptions of personal experiences at the time of a nationally significant event and our recollections of it several months later differ significantly for many. What's interesting is that we usually have rearranged history, but still remember it just like it was yesterday. Researchers Talarico and Rubin conclude: "Flashbulb memories are not special in their accuracy, as previously claimed, but only in their perceived accuracy."[2] This rearranging creates a problem for determining credible court testimony, but helps the rest of us realize that our personal history is made up of what is real and what is vividly imagined. In this chapter, we learn how to shape time to create greater happiness and success—understanding, of course, that it's all in our heads.

Timeliness and Timelessness

How often time is taken for granted! Yet each precious moment falls like a grain of sand in an hourglass. We generally think of time as past, present, and future, but Einstein admits this distinction is "a stubbornly persistent illusion." The ancient Greek language acknowledged time's fluidity by distinguishing two kinds: *chronos* is numeric or chronological time while *kairos* is literally "the right or opportune moment," signifying a time lapse, a moment of indeterminate space in which everything happens. Left brain linear time keeps the physical world on schedule, while right brain *kairos* determines how we experience it. Although chronological history is fact, we can shape it in opportune ways. Time is relative.

Updated Identity

"Memory is identity," writes the British author Julian Barnes in his memoir *Nothing to Be Frightened Of.* He explains: "You are what you have done; what you have done is in your memory; what you remember defines who you are."[3] However, when a painful experience gets stuck in repeat mode, it does not define your true self. Instead, you feel constantly reinjured, regardless of reality. One's true nature is uncovered when these undigested memories are located, processed, and integrated. You saw this in action in the stories of Mike, Carla, and Donna. They each dissolved the inner chaos of past pain and reclaimed their natural strength and spunk.

The Power of Regenerated Memory

In a crisis, the body releases stress hormones to help us secure safety through action. But if movement is thwarted, we get stuck in helplessness and immobilization. These same stress hormones sent to be helpful now turn back on the body and create the fight/flight and freeze response.[4] We regain a sense of safety by regenerating images of the past with actions that defend and protect ourselves and others.

Creating safe memory requires four conditions:

- an environment of safety and resourcefulness
- the freedom to move and act
- the freedom to speak freely
- a present-moment experience

In Carla's real-life story, Buddha provided a safe environment for her to protect her sister and confront their father. Carla now has a newly felt experience of being free, capable, and assertive.

In 2000, a young graduate student discovered that recalling a memory destabilizes it by unlocking the spaces between neurons, leaving it in a vulnerable state to be regenerated.[5] It's similar to unlocking the icons on your smartphone screen by pressing on one until they all jiggle. Once unlocked, we can move and delete icons however we choose. We relock the screen by tapping the smartphone button; when the jiggling stops, it's locked again. In the same way, when we press on a specific memory by seeing it in present time, we unlock it. Once unlocked, the memory is available to redo and relock.

Harvard psychologist Daniel Schacter discovered that remembering and imagining activate many of the same brain circuits, which demonstrates how RIM works so effectively.[6] Both memory and imagination allow us to put ourselves in a time and place other than the one we actually occupy. Thus, imagination can generate new images on top of what's remembered. Carla now feels the freedom and personal power to protect her sister even though she knows what actually happened; the old memory has been reconstructed and loses its power to generate guilt and pain unconsciously.

Asking Your Imagination for a Number

Since critical aspects of a painful memory are implicit (unconscious and nonverbal), the logical mind cannot locate the exact past moment that has injured one's psyche. Therefore, we engage with our imagination to identify the charged event. Detached from left brain logic, the right brain imagination scans memory for a critical number and a specific image. Now the specific time and place that need to be regenerated become visible. Imagination is the perfect seer because these highly charged recollections are subjective; sometimes they are seemingly innocuous moments. What is experienced as traumatic for one person may be manageable for another. For example, Donna was traumatized by a fifth-grade boy calling her ugly. Such an event is not unusual among immature fifth-graders, but her vulnerability made the comment stick.

When we reveal this stuck emotional memory without reliving the pain, it is like locating a buried land mine from a war long over. We pinpoint the specific location and remove it safely without detonating it.

Olivia is a gorgeous brunette in an interesting quandary. She's thirty years old and ready to marry, but she can't decide between two men. Both have proposed, and she's terrified of making a horrible mistake. Closing her eyes and settling into her body, she senses "spinning through the sky" and a dramatic landing similar to Dorothy in the *Wizard of Oz*. Looking at her feet, she sees old-woman shoes. She is also confused by the unfamiliar surroundings. After exploring, she discovers several children and pauses to identify their relationship to her. They are her grandchildren. Allowing her imagination to fill in the blanks, she realizes she's projected into her eighties and can recall that her marriage didn't work. She sees clearly the reasons why.

Next she asks her imagination for a number of the root experience that caused her to select the wrong partner, and she gets "eleven." Ah, with the image of her eleven-year-old self she recalls the time when her mother divorces her dad. Her mom is working constantly, and Olivia is frequently home alone.

Eleven-year-old Olivia voices her feelings to her mom:

Why have you done this to us, Mom? Now you're working all the time to make ends meet. Not only have I lost my dad, I'm losing you. You never spend time with me. I hope I'm never like you. I'll know whom I love, and I'll make it work so I can be with my children.

Mom receives what Olivia has said like a stream of colored energy in her body and responds:

Liv, I'm so sorry. I didn't know you felt this way. I want you to tell me when you feel these things. I know I've been very busy getting my career launched and I've left you alone a lot. I'm really sorry. I love you and enjoy being with you. Would you give me another chance?

Adult Liv also speaks to the eleven-year-old Liv:

Liv, it's so good to remember how spunky you are. I'm proud of you. I know it seems stupid that Mom doesn't see the big picture. Now that I'm grown-up, I understand relationships and feelings are not as simple as they seem. They're complicated. Maybe you and I can help Mom so she feels more confident. That'd probably make us feel better too!

The young Liv receives all that her adult self has expressed like a wave of energy entering her head and flowing through her body. Feeling more centered and safe, she looks at the adult Liv and trusts her; she's even proud of her.

With adult Olivia supporting her, young Olivia turns and speaks to Mom:

Mom, I'm sorry I've been impatient and irritable. Your decision to divorce isn't what I envisioned for my life, and I guess I haven't been very understanding. I realize now that adult relationships have a lot more to them than I thought. The movies make it seem obvious, but I guess not. I want you to know I love you and support you to do what you need to do to feel good about yourself. I'm fine, and now I know I grow up to be a pretty cool woman.

Mom and Olivia (both young and adult) hug. As Olivia returns her focus to her adult self, she now knows the best choice for a husband. She tries the decision on by asking her imagination for a movie of their life together, and it feels just right. The movie anchors in her heart. As her eyes open, she is elated that her indecision is gone. She knows which person she wants to spend her life with. Her confidence is radiant.

Olivia's story demonstrates how anything can happen in our imagination. The adult, eighty-year-old, and eleven-year-old Liv each bring valuable information to the table to make a life-altering decision. We are timeless.

Similarly, fifty-three-year-old Mia realizes she is poised for a quantum leap to greater career success and is afraid. The fear expresses in constant procrastination. When asked for a number of the first time she felt this, her imagination flashes forty-five to forty-seven. Mia is surprised because she has experienced a couple of RIM journeys back to her childhood; she doesn't remember anything significant about her middle age. Imagining the forty-five-year-old Mia, she describes her as a "girly and naive" woman with a career, "playing at life and giving away [her] power to whoever wants or needs it." Mia notices how "helpful" this self needs to be, even to her own detriment. She is willing to support her friends' professional success at the expense of her own.

As Mia moves her attention into her forty-five-year-old self, she speaks for the fears sensed in her body: "I'm afraid of not doing things right and having others be critical." When she seeks out this specific energy in her body, it's a "dark pressure on her right arm as it lies against her belly in a protective position." Bringing a virtual resource with her into this pressure, she further senses a fear about greater success making her "unhappy, tired, and worn out." As she and her virtual resource rest in the energy, it lightens, the darkness dissolves, and her favorite color replaces it.

Once she has defused this negative energy, Mia is free. She looks back at her forty-five-year-old self and notices a shift. She's unattached from the approval of others. In this newly evolved scene, a spot on the floor catches her attention. When she picks the spot up, she finds it holds her lifetime of limiting beliefs about success, and she happily throws it away.

Weeks later, she reports her procrastination has disappeared and she's choosing to step out professionally in a new relaxed way that also supports having a healthy life. She feels really good and unafraid of success. In fact, she's excited! Mia demonstrates how the perfect moment shows up relative to the issue regardless of what the intellect thinks. Your emotional system is smarter than you've known!

People go to various times in their lives, and it's not always painful. Sometimes their imagination takes them to joyful and loving times where they feel capable of achieving anything they want.

For example, during a group demonstration, Callie, a twenty-one-year-old woman, wants to know why she is depressed. She goes initially to her four-year-old self living with her playful Australian family, where she romps outside all day and loves feeling "carefree." This carefree feeling is an orange, bright energy throughout her little body. Immersing herself in this lovely orange energy, she looks outward to view the rest of her life. Her virtual mentor shows her when everything changes: it is at her graduation from high school. Callie remembers the conflict between herself and her mother about going to college. She succumbs to her mom's wishes and is now in school. In this review, her imagination shows that doing something (attending college) in opposition to the intuitively right choice for her is the cause of her depression. Callie is amazed and relieved when she speaks honestly to her mom during this journey. She remarks how good it feels to understand why she was depressed and that she wasn't crazy. Afterwards, several women in the audience thank her for helping them become better moms.

I recently guided a group of 250 people through a RIM process. Accompanied by unique virtual mentors back to a significant time, the vast majority reported an experience of "phenomenal" healing. The few who got stuck in resistance or weren't ready simply went to sleep or nothing happened. Given the choice, the unconscious avoids going where it doesn't feel safe or ready. If your instinct tells you not to go into a memory, always listen and respect it. Never push. Remember, this is an organic process that taps into our natural emotional operating system, and we are careful not to override it. Resistance is welcome here just like every other emotion.

If you have a history involving abuse, you can be supported through the process by a certified RIM facilitator or a therapist with RIM training.[7] The RIM process is not intended for people with mental illness.[8]

Healing at an Intergenerational Level

The timeless quality of imagination lets us generate past, present, and future experiences for powerful healing. Over the last twenty years of originating and refining RIM, I've discovered we can facilitate intergenerational healing where emotional memory related to previous generations is regenerated with profound benefits.

Marie is a beautiful forty-year-old woman who has been living an upper-middle-class life as a stay-at-home mom with a daughter in private school. When serious illness hits her husband and he's unable to work, their financial resources disappear. Marie defuses her anxiety with compulsive shopping.

When Colorado RIM facilitator Dr. Anita Sanchez meets Marie, she and her daughter are living in their car. Her husband has died, Marie's never worked, and there's no money. Anita offers Marie a pro bono session through a local nonprofit. Sitting at a computer in the city library, Marie connects with Anita through Skype. Neither have a clue of the immense depth and breadth of the emotional story about to unfold.

Scanning her body with her eyes closed, Marie senses a large mass that's heavy on her heart and hurting her back and neck. As she moves her attention into this mass, she senses stairs going down into darkness. Walking with a virtual resource (Star) down the stairs, Marie finds and recognizes her three-year-old self.

In this scene, little Marie wakes up and notices her baby brother in bed with her. He isn't breathing, and she starts to cry. She recalls that her parents had been drunk and ignored the newborn, who was crying incessantly the night before. Marie sobs out: "I got the baby in bed with me because I didn't want my baby to cry."

Now her mom and dad are crying and yelling: "You killed the baby! You killed the baby!" and the toddler is sobbing and Mom is screaming. Star protects Marie and brings in a virtual resource for Mom—an angel named June. Mom doesn't want to talk with Marie, so facilitator Anita guides June to turn Mom toward her past. Mom and June walk back in time until four-year-old Mom appears. She has been raped by a neighbor, but doesn't tell: "I can't talk about it because they won't believe me." Feeling distress, the four-year-old asks June to hold and sing to her, and she remembers the feeling of "being loved." As little Marie witnesses Mom's experience, she asks her virtual resource Star to hold her, too. Marie's body shares the experience of feeling loved also.

When Anita asks, "What wants to happen now?" an image of Marie's dad appears. He is also turning toward his past. A virtual resource is called for him, and a wizard with a long white beard appears. The wizard guides Dad to the secluded rural house where he lived as a four-year-old. The little boy Dad sees a man trying to break into his bedroom window. He picks up his bat and strikes at the intruder, which causes the window glass to fall and impale him. The police arrive, and the little boy's parents hush him with "Don't say anything." He's scared and shaking but must be quiet. Ignored by his parents, the little boy is furious that no one is taking care of him.

The little boy turns into Marie's father again, and he faces his tearful daughter: "I'm sorry, Marie. It was a lot of pain for you to carry for so long."

Little Marie speaks to Anita: "I want to be grown-up again." Suddenly she shouts: "OMG, I feel it." "What are you feeling?" asks Anita. "I'm feeling joy. I'm happy my daughter is born and I'm afraid I'll hurt her, but I don't." With tears flowing out of her closed eyes, Marie names joyful times, like walking with her husband and feeling his love: "I've lived most of my life not knowing the happiness that was there, but I'm feeling it now: it's big, big, big joy!" Anita guides Marie to receive the joy like a stream of colored energy flowing into her body, flooding her cells, filling her up, and feeling so good. Marie's face transforms. Her cheekbones are higher, and there are fewer wrinkles around her eyes.

She's glowing as she remembers many happy times: "My husband died, but I was so loved and I love him." As joy flows into her body like a stream of colored energy, she sits in it as long she wants, which is a very long time. "It's good for now," she says as she opens her eyes.

She and Anita sit in silence for a while. Then Marie remarks: "I haven't talked to my parents for twenty years. I didn't know all these things happened to them when they were young. I'm going to get a hold of them. I'm afraid of their rejection, but I have to do this for me."

Six months later, Anita is at a party given by wealthy friends and runs into Marie. She and her daughter are the caterers, and Marie stands in the kitchen looking lovely with coiffed hair. At the end of the evening, Marie tells Anita: "So much has happened since that session, I feel so good, the whole thing about feeling joy is still present." She glances at her daughter.

"I called my parents to tell them what I'd experienced, and at first they were mad and asked me 'How did you know that?' I said, I looked and it was inside me, and they acknowledged it was true. We've talked a couple times since, but the biggest thing is she's graduating," she says as she puts her arm around her daughter.

Marie's daughter tells Anita:

I don't know what you did to my mom, but when she came out of the library, she was different. I could talk with her. In the past, the afraid Mom would have been clingy. Now when I told her I don't want to go to college because I want to do the Peace Corps, she asked: "What do we need to do?"

Anita runs into Marie and her daughter two years later. Marie is working and has a home. Her daughter is preparing for college after returning from a stint in Africa with the Peace Corps.

As in Marie's story, intergenerational healing happens through the client sensing the feelings and events of previous generations. Imagination acts as intuitive translator, which proves remarkable, as you witnessed above. In other words, the client looks from the eyes of parents, ex-spouses, or significant others back at their painful pasts. After these generational characters have safely done and voiced whatever needs to happen, they turn back to the client and share: "What I realize now is . . ."

Clients sometimes know historical details and sometimes not; imagination fills in all important blanks. The process facilitates remarkable inner shifts that create compassion for themselves and those who have hurt them. The offender frequently evolves into asking the client for forgiveness. For example, I've worked with clients who have redone emotional pain through the eyes of their parents/grandparents during World War II and the Holocaust as well as other wars. This resides in us as the carriers of our lineage. We can stop holding unconscious family trauma and dysfunction in our bodies. This more complicated level of work is best undertaken with a facilitator.

Intergenerational healing may seem far-out, but recent research at Emory University School of Medicine in Atlanta demonstrates how induced fear in mice parents is biologically passed to their offspring. Dias and Ressler conditioned mice to fear the smell of cherry blossoms and tested their next two generations. The offspring showed an increased behavioral sensitivity to the scent of cherry blossoms, but not to other odors. Sperm from the conditioned parent was found to have changes to the gene Olfr151. In other words, emotional experiences created chemical changes to the parents' DNA and influenced the genetic makeup of future generations.[9]

In 2014, the American Journal of Psychiatry shared the first study to find intergenerational transmission of the effects of PTSD in the offspring of Holocaust survivors.[10] In reverse, it becomes conceivable that regenerated visceral memories induced through the process of RIM could change one's DNA and influence offspring. Perhaps the emotional work we complete isn't just for us. Maybe it's also for future generations.

Anchoring a Successful Memory Redo

Jung believed the unconscious to be made up of images that are full of meaning and purpose. He suggested the unconscious is constantly dreaming, yet we do not sense these images unless we turn our attention inward. Jung worked with clients to use their creative imagination to address their issues. In his words:

> When you concentrate on a mental picture, it begins to stir, and the image becomes enriched by details. It moves and develops . . . and so when we concentrate on our inner pictures, our unconscious will produce a series of images, which makes a complete story.[11]

Jung described images as having a life of their own with their own logic, provided the conscious mind doesn't interfere.

The RIM process guides imagination to project a successful future of what life looks like now that the sabotaging memories have been dissolved and transformed. What shows up is remarkable. Recently, a client came in wanting to distill her anxiety over launching an exciting new career. She initially experienced an emotional release relative to the deaths of her mom and brother when she was twenty years old that had left her feeling overwhelmingly responsible for her whole family. When this emotional redo was complete, we asked her imagination for a video of what her next six months would look like now that she's free. Her inner screen displayed a vivid movie of effortlessly building her new nonprofit, attracting investors, and expanding services. Later she wrote: "Everything is happening exactly as I saw it."

When imagination reveals the new potential, we have a conscious choice to make important changes or edits. For example, a professional named Paul saw himself returning to his previously "cold and uncaring" government job being more relaxed and playfully interacting with his manager and coworkers rather than waiting for them to engage him, which felt empowering and created a warmer feeling. Asked if there was anything he wanted to add, delete, or edit, he remarked that he wanted to broaden the scope of his new reality to include his social life. Asking his imagination to rewind and revise the future memory, it replayed a lighter, more socially and professionally engaged Paul. Returning to work, he felt less victimized and more successful. Soon he was asked to lead a project, and he started dating after a three-year hiatus.

When I first worked with Jack Canfield ten years ago, I learned about the brain's GPS, the reticular activating system (RAS).[12] Programming your RAS occurs when you imagine living future images as if they're happening now.

When you imagine, you feel viscerally that what is happening is in the present time. It's common to have dramatic experiences because it feels real—similar to dreaming. Rewinding, jumping into the new movie/memory, and living it seven times further imprints it. The empowering memory is integrated at three levels: 1) your conscious mind, 2) your unconscious, and 3) your body (viscera). Now you organically enact this vision without thinking about it. Your brain's RAS is programmed like a GPS and calls attention to things and ideas that will help you have what you've imagined. Your motivation is automatically increased to do things that will help you succeed.

Wolfgang Taube at the University of Fribourg, Switzerland, and other colleagues found that the same brain regions activate whether we imagine engaging in a physical balancing task with closed eyes or we actually execute the same task with open eyes. They further found that passively watching a video of the balancing activity did not activate the same brain areas unless the observer imagined being the person in the video.[13] Thus, your brain equally imprints the experience in memory when you imagine yourself engaged in action or physically enact it. When you imagine being in a regenerated memory of your past or future, you build body memory. Once we have a memory, the mind and body organically duplicate it.

Paul wanted to expand his social life further in a later RIM. He's in his early forties, single, and never married. As he relaxes with his eyes closed for the goal of generating an updated future, his imagination brings up spontaneous images of being married to a blond woman on a farm. Viscerally feeling the caring and tenderness between them is an exhilarating experience and extremely compelling; it's the first time he's felt a deeply tender love. Experiencing the joy of sharing his life in a committed relationship is unfamiliar and very satisfying—more than he realized was possible. His heart opens, his head clears, and his body lightens. After this felt experience of love, he's keen to recreate it in a committed relationship and joins eHarmony. A year later, he reports he is engaged to a blond woman, who, interestingly enough, grew up on a farm.

Imagination and the Body

Humans are remarkable beings, and we've only just begun to uncover the power of imagination and the body. In 2002, Baylor School of Medicine physician Dr. Bruce Moseley experimented with the effectiveness of two different surgical methods to reduce knee pain by shaving damaged cartilage and removing inflammatory material in the knee joint.[14] He added a placebo group as a control. This group received "fake surgery" with sedation and three standard incisions; the surgeon talked and acted as if it were real surgery.

The findings were beyond his expectation. His goal was to discover which surgical technique was more effective, but the most astounding result showed that the patients who received placebo surgery achieved the same level of improvement as those who underwent actual surgery. So as not to interrupt the placebo benefits, these findings weren't released for two years, during which time the media filmed people in the placebo group doing things they couldn't before, like walking and playing basketball.

Recent research at the University of Colorado found that placebos sometimes continue to provide relief even when patients learn the truth. Researcher Scott Schafer explains that study patients became conditioned to believe the placebo relieved pain after four placebo experiences. With conditioned learning, the brain continued to respond as if it were a real treatment even when the patient intellectually knew it wasn't.[15]

How lucky it is we have the ability to reimagine painful, unhappy, and self-sabotaging experience with new imprints in the brain and nervous system. A RIM client once described her previous traumatic experience: "It's like seeing this once painful memory as an antique painting hanging in my life museum. I walk by and recognize, 'Yes that happened, but it no longer has any life to it, it's merely a picture.'"

PRACTICE IT YOURSELF

In the following continuous activity, you will be guided through asking for the age of a "source event," updating that event with a new positive outcome, and finally anchoring that event in a new future. You can do this activity in your mind (with eyes open or closed) or on paper as you go. Or you and a friend can guide each other through the process. Begin by writing down a question or issue about which you'd like greater insight.

Asking for the Age of a Source Event

- Settle into a relaxed physical and mental state in a private location where you won't be disturbed.

- Focus on your breathing, and imagine each breath coming in through the crown of your head and exhaling through the palms of your hands and the soles of your feet. Engage in this breathing until you feel greater relaxation.

- As your attention drops down into your belly, ask your imagination for a number. Receive whatever pops into your awareness first, letting go of any desire to edit. (Remember: this is a creative activity not a thinking one.)

- Your imagination now brings up for you an image of yourself at this age. Notice all the details of this specific image—like what you're wearing, the length of your hair, etc.

- Look into the eyes of this self, and notice what emotion is present.

- Looking at the surrounding environment, you sense this time and place.

Updating a Memory with a New Positive Outcome Activity

- Imagine being the age of the you your imagination has brought up and look out of these eyes. Call in a virtual mentor to be with you, and welcome the first wise, loving, and powerful mentor to show up. (If needed, call in additional virtual mentors till you feel safe.) Notice the appearance and location of mentors in relation to you.

- Still looking from these younger/older eyes, notice that your virtual resource is creating an indestructible protective energy field around you. Notice its color and quality.

- When you feel safe, an image or name of whom you need to speak to pops into your mind.

- A virtual resource also shows up for the person to whom you are speaking.

- Feeling everyone is safe, express (aloud or written) what you want to say and do, while your virtual resource protects and assists you. Take whatever time you need or want to complete speaking/writing what wants to be expressed and acting to do what you want to do in safety.

- Notice how you feel after it's done.

Anchoring the New Memory in the Future Activity

- Your virtual resource shows you a magical movie of how you are different over the next month (now that this memory has been changed). . . . You notice how you look, sound, walk, and talk differently.

- After watching this movie, make any desired changes by rewinding and asking your virtual mentor to create a revised edition, which magically incorporates these changes.

- As you receive the perfect future movie, rewind it, jump into character, and live it seven times.

- Notice how this feels and write notes about the new movie and the new feeling.

- Find this new feeling in your body, and notice the color and texture.

- As you move your attention into the color and immerse yourself, feel it spread throughout your body.

You are timely and timeless
Reclaiming the power to direct your life
You engage your body, mind, and spirit
Artist of the past, present, and future

DO IT!
Dip-See-Do

Do not go where the path may lead, go instead where there is no path and leave a trail.

—Ralph Waldo Emerson

If we did all the things we are capable of doing, we would literally astound ourselves. —Thomas A. Edison

More powerful than all the armies of the world, is an idea whose time has come. —Victor Hugo

Now that you understand how the previous seven steps work practically and scientifically, this chapter simplifies them into an inventive three-part process, which awakens your natural vibrancy and confidence. Unleashing your inner resourcefulness and personal power in this way quickly heals, solves problems, and identifies wise decisions.

ROBERTA'S STORY: CLEARING PAINFUL MEMORIES HEALS

A distressed female voice speaks: "This is Roberta. I'm dying with stage IV cancer and I don't feel ready to go. I'd like to schedule a session to get ready." Roberta's husband David delivers her for the session. He's relinquished his job to spend their final months together. David, a pharmacist, explains their disbelief at the diagnosis of stage IV cancer seven months after a normal colonoscopy.

Interestingly, the doctor diagnoses Roberta's condition only a couple months after her mother's death. Roberta sobs out: "I can't live without my mom. The only good thing about this cancer is I get to be with her again. I can't wait for that."

In her initial session, Roberta dips into body awareness and lands in the middle of terrible physical and emotional pain. Her mother appears in her imagination, and Roberta is comforted. Asking her imagination for a number, she gets seventeen—her age when her mom divorces her dad and leaves Roberta with him. She feels abandoned to figure out graduation and college by herself. Still, it's hard to be furious with the person who is her primary caregiver, the one who loves her the most.

A virtual mentor is summoned, and Jesus appears. Supported by Jesus, teen Roberta speaks to Mom:

> Mom, I can't believe you are leaving. How could you do this to me? I'm just seventeen years old; I'm not ready to run my life. You know Dad isn't going to help. He's consumed with himself and he's upset with your leaving; he's always been selfish. Couldn't you wait one year, please! (She sobs.) All you are thinking about is you. What about me? What about my needs? I'm not old enough for this. I feel inadequate, alone, and scared. I don't know where to start or where to turn.

Roberta then moves her attention into Mom and speaks for her:

> Roberta, I'm so sorry you are hurt. You have always seemed so capable—more capable than I am. I sometimes feel inept around you, so I didn't think it would make any difference to you if I was away. After raising four children and living with a man who ignores me, I feel completely depleted, empty with nothing to give.

Roberta senses the "depleted" feeling in Mom's body for her; her heart looks like a "black blob." Roberta and Jesus move to the blob for Mom, and it quickly fades. Roberta continues to speak for Mom:

> Roberta, I'm so sorry I haven't been available to you. By the time I raised your siblings, I ran out of steam. I feel better now that we are talking. I want to support you. How can we work this out? I feel I must move away, but I could be available. What would be helpful?

Roberta returns her attention to herself and responds: "It feels so much better that you are talking and listening to me, Mom." She is guided to find this feeling of being "listened to" in her body. It's a pervasive pink energy. Moving into it, she embraces it fully and continues speaking:

> It would be very helpful if we could talk on the phone daily for a while as I am deciding about what college to attend. I can't believe you think I'm more capable than you. I've always felt you were brilliant and the woman I want to be like. If you could listen and ask me questions to help me make decisions, that would be great. And if you could go with me when I move into the dorm, it would feel so much less scary.

Mom receives all that has been expressed like a stream of white energy and responds: "Roberta I can do that. Yes, of course. We'll chat each day, and I'll help you move into the dorm. It's a deal. I want you to know, Roberta, I love you dearly. It isn't you I'm leaving—it's your father."

Returning to her own awareness, Roberta responds to Mom: "I love you Mom. I'm so happy. I can handle Dad, I'm his favorite. I feel so much better. Thank you."

After this session, Roberta's tumor markers drop. Over the next four months, she engages in two more RIM processes: one in which she deals with her dad and another in which she deals with her husband's family. In each process she feels victimized and helpless to influence them. In both sessions, she shifts into speaking assertively and finds common ground. Soon she reports the cancer is in remission and her chemotherapy is reduced to a "preventive" level. Further, her relationships with her husband's family have improved significantly—she is elated.

I see her a year later when she brings a referral. Her body has regained its vibrancy, and she looks healthy and confident. Life is good!

Roberta's remarkable recovery demonstrates how quickly physical illness can arise and how quickly it can retreat. It was only two months after her mother's death and seven months following a clear colonoscopy when she was diagnosed with cancer. Even I was surprised that she was in remission after three sessions over four months.

People with the same severity and kind of cancer respond differently to the same treatment. What makes the difference? Could our unconscious emotional state be the influential factor? I remember doing a session with a young woman whose mother had arranged it because she was having surgery in a few days for recurring cancer. During the session, I was concerned when the daughter was unable to receive her father's love and suggested she immediately engage in further deep work, but she was resistant to this option also. During her surgery, she found out the spread of cancer was severe and the outlook was not hopeful.

Another women with ovarian cancer arranged RIM work immediately following her surgery. Initially, I noticed her imagery was spiritual and superficial without deepening into her body. Sharing my concern, she eventually delved into body sensation instead of floating as a transparent figure. When she allowed herself to experience her body sensations, she realized she had no awareness of her sexual organs and lower body. With the safety provided by virtual mentors, she sank further into body awareness and began to do very deep, emotional work. Once she engaged in this work, she commented how good it felt to have awareness of her body—to know who she is and where she is in each moment. She has remained cancer-free.

My observations over twenty years and the latest research show strong connections between earlier emotional pain and later medical problems, suggesting that clearing past painful memories helps the body heal and thrive.

JAMES'S STORY: EXPRESSING NEEDS HELPS A PAINFUL HIP

Have you noticed how a constant ache can become torture? The unrelenting irritant can drive you crazy. James has a left hip that's killing him. A social worker in his mid-fifties, he's been living in Florida with his wife for nine months. Wishing to create a more relaxed lifestyle in preparation for retirement, they've sold their home, left extended family, and relocated to paradise. Things haven't gone smoothly, and their dream of a laid-back life is fading. Instead, James is working harder than ever.

A physical therapist, a doctor, and a chiropractor have all treated James for his hip pain, but there has been no change. When he hears that RIM facilitator Michael Kline is offering sessions, James is interested.

Tracking his body awareness, James is drawn to the pain, which forms an oblong snakelike shape that's dark red, flexible, and moving. When he dialogues with the pain, it tells him that leaving behind his secure job, children, and extended family is harder than expected. There's a frustration and sadness building in his body that he's not there for his family, "dad, brother, and son." Locating the frustration and sadness in his body, he moves into it and asks for a number of the first time he felt this. Seven-year-old Jimmy shows up and connects with his resource teacher/coach Mr. Marks.

Mr. Marks tells Jimmy that he looks out for others more than himself. He coaches little Jimmy to express his forgotten needs rather than help others. Jimmy receives "courage, compassion, encouragement" like a stream of yellow sunlight from his caring coach. He realizes he'll have to slow down and recognize his feelings in order to express them. Anger is the hardest, and he feels "relief" with the thought of being able to share his true feelings with loved ones. Coach expresses confidence in Jimmy, and there's a sudden physical shift. He notices the pain is significantly less than it has ever been. Empowered, he feels in charge of the pain and thankful for its helpful messages. As the pain continues to subside, it tells the adult James that a small amount remains as a reminder to express his feelings, and when he is in balance, it will go away completely. James changes his patterns and begins to take time to do things for himself like exercise and meditation. The pain remains true to its purpose of increasing when he ignores his feelings and decreasing when he takes care of himself.

James is so impressed with his results, he decides to learn the RIM process and use it with his psychotherapy clients.

HARRY'S EXPERIENCE: UNRAVELING ADDICTION

Harry has been sober for more than ten years. He has a professional position and is settled into a new marriage, but his addictive pattern has morphed. He has responded to stress by seeking immediate pleasure—first with alcohol, then shifting to drugs, and now heading underground into sexual addiction.

Sexual addiction can be kept more hidden from public scrutiny than substance abuse through online porn, affairs, masturbation, and sexual fantasy. Nonetheless, his secret is exposed when his unsuspecting daughter opens his office door and catches a glimpse of the online porn. She is horrified and afraid to be alone with him.

Harry's wife immediately insists he leave until he gets help. He sees he will lose everything if he lets this pattern continue, so he engages in RIM sessions. In his first, he relaxes into a meditative state. In his body there's a hot, red ball in his throat, making it difficult to swallow. This ball-shaped energy has a hard outer shell with a gooey black center. Drawn to the center, he imagines himself inside it. Alone in the dark, he feels afraid and suffocated. When he calls on a virtual mentor, his deceased mother appears, and his anxiety eases.

The root experience that arises is a teen brother sitting on seven-year-old Harry trying to make him say "uncle." Harry is unwilling to submit to his brother's control and passively rides out the threat without speaking. A strange contradiction anchors in his young body that giving up his voice and abdicating control to others mean success. Harry's immobilization puts him in his reptilian instinctual or survival brain. "When this system kicks in, all our mental and physical resources are consumed with avoiding death. This brain does not distinguish between emotional or physical annihilation. Trauma researcher Van Der Kolk points out that other people, and we ourselves, cease to matter when this part of the brain takes over."[1] Such unconscious behavior is a hallmark of Harry's addictive behavior. This first RIM session opens his eyes to how his subconscious is running his life without him knowing it.

In a subsequent session, a scared four-year-old Harry hides around the corner while his same older sibling and his dad get into a violent fight. Hiding from life becomes his pattern. Little honesty or authenticity gets expressed; instead, everything is a game of trying to look good to avoid being found out as scared, weak, or stupid. It's comforting and devastating at the same time. His ego-focused left brain convinces Harry he is clever, when in fact he is merely silencing his authentic self.

As Harry becomes aware of this dual life (public and inner), his sexual addiction significantly diminishes, yet sexual fantasy remains a primary way to numb uncomfortable and bored feelings. Thus he slides under the radar with this secret until his family and boss once again make it clear his behavior is not working. When Harry realizes that he cannot get by with any sexually addictive behavior, he hits bottom and understands for the first time that he's been hiding rather than taking responsibility for himself. He faces the reality that he is sneaking through life and blaming others whenever he gets negative feedback—which he gets regularly. Though he attends AA programs, sponsors others, and connects weekly with his own sponsor, his sexual fantasies have continued to interrupt his effectiveness at work and in relationships.

About this time, a RIM session reveals an image of a young boy who realizes he has a "conscience." This inner process reveals that Harry's been rejecting his conscience to avoid the self-condemning feelings that arise when he acts without integrity.

Harry isn't taking responsibility for the behavior that gets him in trouble because he's working excessively to make himself feel better after he feels bad from acting poorly. This destructive hide-and-seek allows him to get by, but not thrive.

As Harry's self-awareness continues to expand, he realizes the high cost of his slippery behavior—the destruction of his self-esteem. He commits to rebuild self-respect by consistently acting with "honesty and diligence" by eliminating the one remaining symptom of frequent sexual fantasy. To keep himself honest, he sets up several ways to receive feedback both at home and at work, including the monitoring of his digital devices for porn activity and an annual lie detector test.

With his greater self-awareness and these changes in place, Harry's family experience him as significantly more emotionally connected with them and forgive him for the past. He finds a new level of authenticity by communicating his vulnerabilities rather than hiding them to appear smart. His primary intention is to be 100 percent present, and his habit of seeking immediate pleasure when stressed or bored is traded for the self-respect and maturity gained from facing life's challenges. Hopefully, this new willingness to face issues will become an automatic healthy habit. Until then, he must stay alert, responsible, and seeking feedback. Harry wisely hires an addiction coach to help.

Harry's story illustrates the critical difference between constructive imagery and addictive fantasy. It's all about reality. RIM imagery is used to create a healthier reality, while addictive fantasy persistently avoids reality. When sexual fantasy is used as a habitual way to avoid life, we don't face or work through issues. Because no one knows what's happening, the only visible symptom is a lack of connection and follow-through on agreements. In other words, we retreat into our own world where no one can hurt us—or love us.

Harry also demonstrates how sexual addiction is a complex and persistent problem that frequently goes unchecked until one's life falls apart. A combination of community (addiction support groups), individual, and family treatment is most effective. *The 30-Day Sobriety Solution* by Jack Canfield and David Andrews is a very helpful tool that offers solutions and online methods to change addictive behavior. They provide one of the most comprehensive recovery resources ever published.[2]

Central to changing any addiction is the reworking of early traumatic experiences with RIM or similar techniques to develop a deeper emotional understanding that motivates self-compassion and committed change. Both right brain emotional healing and left brain willpower are indicated.

ALAN'S STORY: HEALING THROUGH THE HEART NOT THE HEAD GETS GREATER RESULTS

Alan is a bright, young filmmaker. He's talented and loves the work, yet his company isn't growing because he can't trust others to help him. He consciously wants to expand the volume of projects, but is uncomfortable delegating; the turnaround time is tediously slow.

When a RIM facilitator negotiates a trade for video work, Alan gains a session. With his eyes closed, his stomach calls his attention. He feels like vomiting and begins to cry. When he asks his imagination for the source of the tears, an image of his childhood dog Max appears, and Alan feels deep sadness. He remarks that Max's love is what he trusts most, and the dog's spirit becomes Alan's virtual resource.

With Max by his side, Alan finds the energy of "not trusting" and goes deeper into the nauseated feeling in his gut. An image appears of six-year-old Alan on a fishing outing with his parents. The exact scene is when he loses hold of his fishing pole and his dad is mad. Losing the expensive rod is a big deal because finances are tight. Dad speaks harshly to the six year-old: "You should know better. If I want something done right, I have to do it myself. I can't trust anyone. Alan you have to learn to do things right. You're old enough now."

Alan is crying and feeling sad that Dad is so furious with him. Finding this sadness in his little body, he embraces it, and through tears he apologizes: "Dad, I'm so sorry, I didn't mean to lose the pole. It just slipped through my hands. I don't even know how." Sitting in the sadness, Alan eventually remembers that his dad did apologize when they returned home, and the son speaks again: "Dad, I forgive you. I know you didn't mean to hurt me. You were worried about the money. I understand."

Alan notices Max and feels good remembering his uncon-ditional love. With the lead of "What wants to happen next?" Alan sees himself a couple years younger than his current age of twenty-eight. With virtual Max still by his side, he feels differ-ent, his stomach doesn't hurt, and there's something small in his belly. Bringing Max with him into the belly, Alan discovers an open space that's "sensory not visual." In this openness he feels safe that he can create anything he wants. He and Max romp and play freely until Alan senses Max say: "I love you Alan. You trusted me, and you still do. I went to school with you, and then was free to do whatever I wanted. I was always there for you." Alan tearfully receives the dog's love like a ribbon of light that fills his body with "love and trust." When asked by the facilitator if there is anything else that needs to happen, Alan asks: "Can I keep Max?" Reassured that Max is always filling him with love and trust, the filmmaker opens his eyes.

As he faces the facilitator, Alan is a bit "weirded out" that his experience was so deeply emotional, which he didn't expect. He mentions that "it didn't address my issue of delegating, but I am a perfect ten of feeling loved." A month later, the facilitator receives a call from the colleague who connected them:

I don't know what you did to Alan, but he's totally different. He's gotten two big projects since the session and has hired lots of new people to help him. Oh, and he's fallen in love. He trusts his people such that he's off enjoying free time with his new girlfriend. When he was my student, he never played because he was overly responsible.

....

The intensity of six-year-old Alan's sadness caused his dad's comments to anchor unconsciously in Alan's young brain. Because RIM is a nonintellectual process that produces beneficial results without logical thinking, Alan's mind initially didn't see the connection between his Dad's saying "I can't trust anyone" and his discomfort in delegating. Dipping into his body and allowing imagination to recall and redo this critical moment, however, precipitated an organic change that effectively addressed his stated problem automatically. Alan's story demonstrates how self-limiting thoughts and feelings can be erased and behavioral changes made without intellectual understanding.

HOW IT WORKS—PRACTICALLY AND SCIENTIFICALLY

This chapter includes a description of the essential RIM process, why it works, and how to use it in daily life.

Dip-See-Do

Have you heard the phrase "Is there a 'Kick Me' sign on my back?" from people who are feeling negativity coming at them from every angle? At times, it's true. We are the embodiment of what's saved in our conscious awareness and unconscious. Emotional memory is like a screensaver imprinted on the body and persona. Similar to a computer screensaver, you see it initially, but over time you forget. For example, when Marilyn begins her session with RIM facilitator Madelaine Osborne, she thinks she is overweight because of angry overeating. However, she soon discovers the true source is a forgotten emotional imprint of a seventeen-year-old girl grief-stricken following her mom's death. As the sadness emerges, Marilyn automatically reconnects with her mother's love and senses the change. Weeks later she reports: "I feel like a different person. The food thing has already changed—it was instantaneous. I haven't overeaten since those two sessions, and I'm loving myself again."

People sometimes complain: "I'm doing everything I can. Why isn't it working? I have no idea what I'm doing wrong." Like Marilyn, their emotional screensavers have become invisible but they are still filtering and distorting how these people look at the world and how the world sees them. It creates an impression that's constant until the settings are located, edited, and resaved. The essential RIM process is a way to discover and edit a self-sabotaging screensaver into a success magnet.

Three steps are essential to RIM:

DIP into your inner settings.

SEE the subconscious screensaver and unconscious resources.

DO transformational changes and save them in emotional memory.

DIP

Dipping into the spaces between your thoughts allows you access to subconscious settings and unconscious resources. Imagining your brain waves helps you see how it works. Brain activity moves at various speeds depending on the frequency of thoughts. (See the illustration on page 212.) Beta brain wave activity is rapid thinking that keeps attention focused on the external world; thus, the external world seems like reality. Alpha speed is more relaxed and allows greater connection with your inner world, resulting in mutual awareness of both internal and external realities. Theta activity exists in the twilight state when you're half awake and half asleep. This brain wave reflects a meditative state where you become most suggestible to the unconscious. Delta is the slowest brain wave state and reflects unconscious, restorative sleep. Gamma is a unique brain wave that's the fastest, but indicates the highest states of consciousness and "aha" experiences.[3] We'll talk more about gamma brain waves later.

Imagine gliding down the side of a brain wave from busy beta thoughts into relaxed theta twilight. In this dip between thoughts, you access subconscious and unconscious waters, retrieve healing insights, and bring them up into conscious thought. For clarification, I describe the space between thoughts as having two layers: subconscious and unconscious. The subconscious is just below awareness and contains human thoughts-feelings-beliefs-memories that have been forgotten, repressed, suppressed, avoided, unknown, or ignored. As you dip further into your depths, you discover the unconscious that holds unknown/unrealized creativity, intuition, spiritual insight/resourcefulness, and inherent states of peace and love. Here, you retrieve safe and loving support and brilliant insights and solutions. It's like fishing in a pond with a murky surface and a deep reservoir of sparkling water alive with resourcefulness.

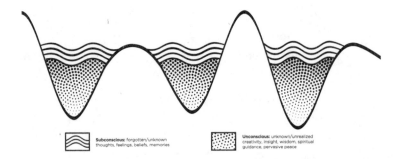

Subconscious: forgotten/unknown thoughts, feelings, beliefs, memories

Unconscious: unknown/unrealized creativity, insight, wisdom, spiritual guidance, pervasive peace

In contrast, worry and rumination are rapid-fire, fearful thinking with little time for dipping between thoughts. Thus, inner resources remain untapped. It's like riding a bucking bronco while trying to solve a mathematical problem. We've all felt like that one time or another!

Interestingly, neuroscientists Kounios and Beeman have used EEG and MRI studies to identify the "aha" moment of sudden insight in the brain. They discovered a burst of gamma-band high-frequency (40 hertz) activity produced insight and was unconsciously preceded by a burst of a slow alpha-band (10 hertz) activity. They suggest the slower alpha band was the brain's way of closing *its* eyes to external stimuli to allow creativity. They label it a "brain blink," since research participants were asked to keep their eyes open. In other words, the naturally occurring slower alpha activity was essential for a burst of sudden elevated insight to happen. Without it, participants in the study demonstrated slower rational problem-solving with their attention focused on the external image. They lacked the brain blink and gamma burst.[4]

This research appears consistent with how RIM works. Closing your eyes and slowing thinking through body and image awareness create a blank mind where your imagination can produce "aha" insights. Since surprise helps the brain retain information, the "aha" images are vividly remembered.

SEE

Neuroscientists agree our vision is like a movie that blends light and sound waves with inner emotional experience into a story that's removed from reality. Our thoughts and feelings inspire our sense of what is real or not. Therefore, revealing emotional screensaver images helps us "see" the subjective filter creating our current reality. Gaining a keener awareness of hidden, sabotaging feelings, thoughts, and beliefs makes them available to be transformed.

During "seeing," imagination becomes the telescope to view the form of unconscious images, feelings, and beliefs in a dramatic, caricature-like way, which makes it easier to get what's really happening. This may take the form of images, voices, feelings, and words. All forms are equally powerful; they come through the right brain *sensing* mode, which perceives in a creative rather than factual manner. On the other hand, the left brain names and measures them.

Rosemary is a physician who has practiced successfully for five years. She's currently earning a specialty certification and has failed the clinical test twice. She has only one more chance to pass. The evaluators who have seen her in action remark that she's not her usual self during testing. When Rosemary closes her eyes and dips beneath the surface, she has no idea what is getting in her way. She is surprised by the initial image of her three-year-old self with her dominating father who demands she "act like an adult." Safety is created with virtual mentors, and little Rosemary speaks her anger to her dad as she grows more confident. She senses spontaneous images of herself at older ages, and she continues to speak honestly to her dad.

HUMAN BRAIN WAVES

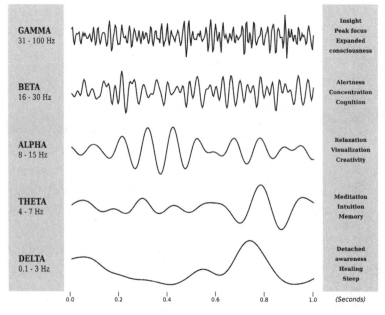

© Artellia | Dreamstime.com

Her imagination guides her through these life experiences until it eventually lands in present time where there's an image of her dad in despair because he has alienated his four children and ex-wife. After bringing in a virtual resource for this suffering dad, there is an enlightening dialogue between him and his virtual resource, and he feels loved for the first time in his life. Dad turns to adult Rosemary and tells her: "Rosemary, I realize now I was too hard on you, and I'm sorry. I never felt the approval of my father, and it influenced how I've parented you. Can you forgive me after all these years?" Rosemary feels compassion for him and is relieved to forgive.

Although Rosemary's well-developed left brain is confused, even disoriented, by this right brain, nonlinear experience, she is pleased to report six weeks later: "I have noticed after the session that I'm not angry with my dad anymore even if I try. This is GREAT!" Furthermore, when the next clinical test for her specialty certification comes up, she pretends she is on the ward or clinic instead of being tested, and it works. She is completely surprised that her experiences with her dad were causing her to fail. Rosemary's story shows how seeing the root cause of an issue is essential to redoing it in a successful way. Her experience is very different from processing her test anxiety intellectually.

DO

Once you *dip* and *see* the original source of a hidden block, the *do* is simple: create safety with virtual resources and speak/write whatever needs to be expressed. This safe experience of being seen and heard along with the freedom to act is profoundly healing. Trauma specialist Bessel Van Der Kolk describes the value of

[an] awareness of our subtle sensory, body-based feelings: the greater that awareness, the greater our potential to control our lives. Knowing what we feel is the first step to knowing why we

feel that way. If we are aware of the constant changes in our inner and outer environment, we can mobilize to manage them.[5]

Do is the step where your imagination creates a new vision of your future now that the past has been transformed, and you have the option to make desired edits. For example, Rosemary finishes her RIM process by watching a new movie of what her life looks like over the two months following her session. Her imagination shows her studying less, relaxing more, and pretending she is her usual doctor self while being evaluated. As you read earlier, this image stuck and came to mind as a spontaneous idea just before entering the exam. Furthermore, Rosemary's body forces her to "study less and relax more" with a brief illness that sends her to bed for three days before the exam. Since Rosemary's mind, body, and spirit have become partners, her body skillfully contributes to implementing her unconscious solution. Our emotional system is smarter than we think!

The Whole Brain Zone

As you've read and experienced throughout this book, the RIM *dip-see-do* process engages both right brain creativity and left brain intellect. The right brain, however, is the leader in this process, contrary to the norm in our left-brain-dominant society. Richard Chi and Allan Snyder of the Centre for the Mind in Sydney, Australia, studied the effectiveness of out-of-the-box problem-solving compared to linear, cognitive problem-solving. To shock problem-solvers out of their left brain dominance, they designed a "thinking cap" that delivered a weak electrical current targeted to disable the left anterior temporal lobe (ATL) and enhance activity in the right ATL. People were three times more likely to solve a complex riddle quickly while wearing the thinking cap.[6] Similarly, RIM turns down the left brain by closing the eyes and engages the right brain through creative imagery, resulting in quicker, more flexible problem-solving.

When the right brain visionary leads with a dream/purpose/solution and the left brain administrator implements it, you evolve whole-brain function.

Left Brain	Whole Brain Zone	Right Brain
administrator	whole person	visionary
physical	curious	imagined
measurable	inventive	felt
logical	creative	intuitive
linear	healing	emotional

The whole brain zone is where genius happens. Throughout history, the most brilliant inventors, researchers, mathematicians, artists, and composers have described the importance of being guided by a strategic combination of creative and logical activity.[7] Jonas Salk, who discovered the polio vaccine, summarizes: "Intuition will tell the thinking mind where to look next." Einstein saw the theory of relativity in an instant as he imagined riding a thunderbolt across the sky; it took him thirteen years to prove it. The Wright brothers imagined flying for years prior to building their first airplane. Both creative visioning and logical execution are essential.

Dr. Robert Freedman is a renowned psychiatric researcher and also a family friend. Following his journey through the years, I've been amazed to notice how this fastidious scientist leaves space for creative coincidences at critical times. When they occur, his logical mind quickly makes use of them. He and his colleagues noticed that frequently hospitalized schizophrenic patients chain-smoke. In fact, 80 percent of them smoke thirty cigarettes per day and extract 50 percent more nicotine than other smokers.[8] It turns out high doses of nicotine diminish sensory input, and that helps these patients focus their attention more effectively. There are negative side effects with nicotine as well, of course.

Bob and his colleagues chose to study an ignored nicotine receptor. When he searched the Internet, he discovered exactly what he thought might work. Research on marine worms done many years earlier by Dr. William Kem called his attention. There was something unusual about the hearts of these worms, which were found to secrete a substance similar to nicotine without the usual side effects. Kem told Bob, "I've been waiting by my phone for this call for ten years." This substance is now being developed into a completely new drug for schizophrenia, and many drug companies are following suit.

The marriage of both sides of the brain in the *dip-see-do* process allows magical things to happen, as you have read in the real-life stories. The right brain creative/emotional/intuitive with the left brain logical/intellectual/grounded aspects team up to find new discoveries, sustain resources, and transform traumatic memory. As Salk said, the right brain intuitive leads while the left brain identifies the details to make everything comprehensible and applicable.

Jill Bolte Taylor is a neuroscientist who suffered a stroke to the area of her left brain that controls executive function. As this region lost function, she struggled to remember how to dial the phone for help. At the same time, her now-dominant right brain took her on an inner journey of beauty and love through an expansive universe. Her right brain experience instilled such inner peace and joy in her that Jill was tempted to lie down and enjoy rather than seeking assistance. Fortunately, she was able to get help.[9] Her experience demonstrates how feelings of love and peace reside in our creative center, while we still need the left brain administrator to survive. The gifts of both right and left hemispheres are unique and essential to health and happiness.

The Brain and Emotional/Physical Pain

Science is rapidly proving that the mind, brain, and body are tightly linked. Ethan Kross and his colleagues from the University of Michigan and the University of Colorado Boulder compared MRI patterns between people feeling heartbreak over a breakup and people suffering with the sensory experience of physical pain. They found that both kinds of pain occupy similar areas of the brain and are equally distressing. The emotional pain, however, lasted longer and could be recalled, while physical pain could not. Though emotional and physical pain register in the body similarly, the long-term effects of emotional pain are actually greater than those of physical pain.[10]

Interestingly, Naomi Eisenberger, an assistant professor of psychology at UCLA, discovered that the brain interprets social rejection as equally harmful as physical injury.[11] Since emotional pain registers in the same area of the brain as physical pain, DeWall actually found that taking Tylenol diminished hurt feelings and social exclusion.[12] (Could this explain the prevalent problem of addiction to prescribed drugs?) In RIM, we've discovered the reverse can work, too. Resolving emotional pain has diminished physical pain and illness. Emotional pain is physical, and physical pain is emotional.

As mentioned in chapter one, our immune function is suppressed by chronic negative emotions. Dr. John Arden, director of training for mental health in Northern California Kaiser Permanente, finds that people who are depressed or lonely get more colds, and people who are depressed in later life get dementia earlier."[13]

Yes, it's true. Taking care of your feelings is taking care of your body!

Natural Charisma

Over the last twenty years, I've noticed people naturally become more charismatic after they clear emotional blocks, attracting more friends, partners, customers, and even strangers. More than once after RIM sessions, surprised clients remark how strangers are drawn to them—a new experience. For some, these interactions have resulted in relationships. Their "personal charm" (the mundane meaning of charisma) is active and attracting others.[14] It's probably no surprise that feeling free and safe creates personal magnetism.

When researcher Stephen Porges introduced the Polyvagal Theory in 1994, he proved that subtle facial and tonal shifts in people are perceived at the unconscious level and organically make us feel either safe or suspicious. These responses are sensed even prior to conscious thought.[15] Details like facial tension, curvature of the lips, and angle of the neck communicate whether someone is comfortable, suspicious, relaxed, or frightened.[16] It explains why a friendly face and soothing voice influence us to feel safe at a gut level.

As you've read in many personal stories, childhood experiences that stimulate feelings of danger may cause us to slide under the radar to keep safe. Redoing these critical times at the neurophysiological level internalizes a feeling of inner safety. This shift helps us to feel comfortable sharing ourselves and attracting others to step closer.

CLOSING

Life reveals itself continuously. We learn, grow, and self-evolve, yet still don't arrive. Unforeseen stresses, illnesses, and events remain, regardless of our best efforts. On the other hand, we can choose a life that evicts perfectionism and comparison. When we allow our inherent state of curiosity to be our primary driver, life gets easier and easier. Like babies exploring the environment, we welcome our immediate experience as a teacher.

When my son Walker was six months old, he had an intussusception, which is a serious and potentially life-threatening condition when the intestine telescopes on itself and blocks the passageway. Fortunately, it was reversed without surgery. When the ER doctor returned to the waiting room to tell us the procedure had been successful, he remarked how intently Walker had watched the x-ray equipment: "I could see his mind curiously working to figure it out." I was amazed he could be more curious than frightened given the circumstances (not true for his parents). He reminded me we are resilient beings and our native curiosity keeps life interesting even when things get tough.

I frequently hear complaints of "I already worked on that emotional issue," as if once we clear an emotion, we're done. The truth is living is a messy business. We accumulate residual feelings in the same way our homes gather dust. You'd never expect a house cleaning to last forever, but we sometimes expect intense emotional work to mean we're finished. Instead, our emotional landscape is similar to our external environment: it requires consistent attention to stay comfortable and attractive.

Applying *dip-see-do* regularly acts like a self-cleaning oven. Doing the activities in the Practice It Yourself sections of this book will keep you on track or get you back on when you've fallen off.

When you look inward, your imagination uses the opportunity to project what's bubbling there given the context of who you are even when you aren't thinking about it. Joan Newsom is a RIM facilitator who uses the process herself and with her high school students. Whenever Joan finds herself feeling less than happy, she sits down and writes through the *dip-see-do* process. She uncovers hidden feelings related to previous experiences that no longer apply. Realizing her feelings are from the past rather than the present allows her to identify and clear old emotions and address what's coming up currently. By the time she's back in the present, her mood has shifted and the issue seems minor—nothing to fret about.

Joan also guides her high school students through a group *dip-see-do* process intended to scare away one's fears. The students have reported shifting from feeling "fear of Mom"—to feeling "comfort"; feeling "scared"—to feeling "freedom"; feeling "scared of the truth"—to feeling "love and adoration"; feeling "alone in a city"—to feeling "confidence"; feeling "weak"—to feeling "oblivion—I can't remember my faults, my failures, only clear oblivion."

Joan guides another class using a group RIM process to imagine looking from the perspective of a character in an assigned literary book. A few students commented:

There are many things I think we as humans overlook, and slowing it down gives us time to think. I enjoyed this process very much and love realizing connections I would never have made otherwise. It is relaxing, as I think this world is too rushed and I need time to think and put everything back into values. I can't thank you enough.

Putting myself into the mind-set of someone else is always quite hard, especially a character in a book who doesn't really exist. However, it always helps me realize how different everyone is and how each person is in search of something else in their life. It really gets me thinking about my journey in life and what the goal is. This exercise is very interesting to do.

I learned how to relax and think creatively.

One of the most inspiring things I learned is that, of course, where you came from does affect you, but it doesn't determine or limit you.

I learned from the process that it is difficult to reflect from just a character and not from yourself. It is quite hard to not add in any of my opinions or background.

What I have learned from this process is the ability to get into character. I think the most important thing was to experience and almost force myself to be in another mindset of a person and realize/understand what they would do. Personally, it opens up new philosophies and ways to think. It is a path to exercise the right side of your brain and play with different ideas but decipher the character at the same time.

....

These students show us how simple dipping into imagination illuminates inner feelings even when the assignment is about someone else. We have an organic emotional operating system designed to grow our self-awareness. We simply need to look inward with childlike curiosity.

PRACTICE IT YOURSELF

You can do this activity in your mind (with eyes open or closed) or on paper as you go. Or you and a friend can guide each other through the process. Begin by writing down a question or issue about which you'd like greater insight.

DIP

- Closing your eyes, tune inward and focus on the inside of your body. Your attention settles down behind your navel as you imagine breathing in and out through it until you are more relaxed.

- Sensing where your attention is drawn in your body, go there. Explore the size, shape, color, movement of this area, etc.

- A virtual resource who wants to support you with this issue shows up. Notice the details of his/her appearance, location, etc.

- You and your virtual resource move into whatever aspect of this energy is most compelling and allow it as much as possible.

SEE

- As you immerse in this energy, your imagination brings up an image that represents this issue.
- Sensing this image, receive whatever shows up, even if it doesn't make sense.
- Noticing all the details, sense how you feel.
- Now moving your awareness into the image, look back at yourself.

DO

- Having moved your awareness into this image and looked back at yourself, sense what the image is here to share with an unedited stream of consciousness of automatic speaking or writing. Spontaneously express what the image wants to say to you, using the following sentence leads. Speak or write what answers intuitively arise into awareness to explore the details:
  - What I'm here to represent and share is . . . because . . .
  - What I know about you is . . .
  - What I know about this issue is . . .
  - What else wants to be shared is . . .
  - How it feels to speak this to you is . . .
- Moving your attention back into yourself, receive all the image has shared like a stream of colored energy, noticing the color and quality of it and where it's entering your body.

- Fully receiving the stream of colored energy, notice how it feels.

- Looking back at the image now, notice if it's gone or has changed form.

- Your imagination creates a magical movie before you of what your coming week looks like now that you have this new awareness. Watch it and notice what's different.

- Rewind the movie and jump into it to imagine living it.

- Notice how this feels: the movie moves into or around your body, or both, and becomes fully available to you.

You Get to Be You
No Matter What Happens
Your Spirit Remembers and Reminds You
Who You Are

SIMPLE AND SPEEDY RIM TOOLS FOR DAILY LIFE

Enjoy this collection of several simple RIM techniques to use in daily life so you can regain the wild joy of naturally being yourself, even when it seems illogical and improbable!

REGRET ERASER

- Identify your regret, narrow it down, and remember the details of the event.

- Closing your eyes, relax into your body.

- As you move your attention into your heart, hear one word describing what you're feeling as you remember this regretful experience.

- Find this feeling in your body, and sense its size, shape, color, and any details of it.

- Your imagination brings in at least one virtual resource to be with you.

- As you move with your virtual resource(s) into the regret energy, you sense an image of whom you need to speak to.

- Speak or write what needs to be voiced to this person. The more you express, the lighter you feel. Continue expressing until your feelings have emptied.

- Ask your imagination to show you a magical movie that regenerates the regret experience, including images of you acting in new, beneficial ways. Receive all the details and feelings as you watch.

- As the movie rewinds, jump into it and live it. Do this six more times until it feels natural.

- Opening your eyes, record or share your experience and how you feel now.

IRRITATION SOOTHER

- Closing your eyes, pay attention to your breathing for several minutes as your attention easily drops into your belly.

- Sense the location in your body of the irritated feeling.

- Notice the quality of this irritated energy: its size, shape, color, movement, and any other details.

- Call in virtual resources and notice who shows up to be with you. Imagine moving into the most disturbed part of this energy with them accompanying you.

- Resting in this energy as best as you can, notice how it changes.

- As you rest in this energy, your virtual mentors share what you are most irritated about. Receive it and allow the feeling.

- Resting in this greater awareness, move into your virtual mentors and from their perspective notice what can be done to help this situation. Take a minute.

- Returning awareness to yourself, notice how you're feeling now.

- When you're ready, write or verbally share your experience and what you have learned.

DECISION-MAKER

- Closing your eyes, take a deep breath to the count of four (1-2-3-4). Hold your breath for the count of four (4-3-2-1). Exhale to the count of four (1-2-3-4). Hold the emptiness for the count of four (4-3-2-1). Continue this breathing pattern as long as you want, as you more fully relax.

- With your right hand extended palm up, ask your imagination to place an image there that reflects a *yes* response to this decision.

- Receive what shows up first, noticing its details.

- Moving into it, dialogue with it to see the consequences of a *yes* decision and how it feels. Take some time.

- With your left hand extended palm up, ask your imagination to drop an image representing the *no* choice there and receive what shows up first, noticing its details.

- Moving into it, sense what it feels like to choose *no* and its outcomes.

- Moving back into yourself, sense the energy of these two choices held in your hands.

- Clap your hands together as your imagination creates a puff of smoke. As the smoke clears, a new image appears that perfectly represents your intuitive answer. Move into this image, and sense all it means.

- Receiving this new image, imagine bringing it to your chest and allowing it to easily move into your heart. Notice how this feels.

- When you're ready, record or share your experience and what you have learned about yourself.[1]

BIG DREAM VIEWER

- Close your eyes and breathe several times in through the front of your heart and out through your upper back.

- As you feel more relaxed, ask your imagination to bring up an image of a safe and loving virtual resource who loves you and supports your greatest vision. Receive whoever pops up first, letting go of any desire to edit.

- As you sense this powerful virtual resource, notice details of appearance and location in relation to you. Move into this resource, and look out of these eyes.

- Looking out from the loving and powerful eyes of the virtual resource, gaze back at yourself and easily sense the big dream/mission/passion that wants to be expressed.

- Your virtual resource creates a detailed movie right before your eyes that reveals what your life looks like as your greatest dream is realized. Observing this movie, notice what's happening in your relationships, work, play, finances, health, and contribution to the world.

- After you've seen all the details, rewind the dream, jump into it, and live it. Take as much time as you need to live all the details. Then rewind it again and live it six more times. The movie has a life of its own, and it evolves and grows. Notice how it feels to live this big dream.

- When you are ready, open your eyes and write down all you saw and experienced, noticing how it feels.

- Share this dream with three or more people and notice how it feels to speak your dream aloud.

VOICE ENHANCER

- Relax into a comfortable space with your eyes closed. Settle in like this spot was created perfectly to fit your unique body.

- As you feel more relaxed, sense in your body where your voice is hiding, and notice the location, size, shape, and color of this hidden voice. You may get specific images. Everything is welcome. Take your time.

- As you sense it, ask your imagination to bring in a virtual resource to travel with you. The two of you move into this energy of a silenced voice.

- As you settle into it, ask your imagination to bring up a number. Openly receive it as the first time you felt this way.

- An image of you at this age appears.

- Imagining being this younger self, look out of these eyes and see who is silencing your voice.

- With your virtual resource acting as a safe force field between you and this person, safely speak or write what wants to be expressed to this person that has never been voiced before. Take whatever time is needed.

- Continue to speak until you are loudly and clearly sharing your voice. Stretch into it. Take as much time as you want or need.

- Notice how this feels in your body.

- Find in your body the new feeling of expressing your clear, loud voice. Notice its location, color, and texture.

- Moving into it, immerse yourself in this *"expressing your voice"* energy, as you swim in it, play in it, and become it.

- Notice how this feels.

- When you are ready, open your eyes and record or share your experience, noting what you learned and how it can help you in your current life.

PROBLEM-SOLVING MAGICIAN

- Identify the problem you want to explore.

- Close your eyes, and take several deep cleansing breaths that carry you deeper into your body and relaxation. Imagine breathing in through the front side of your body and out through the back side of your body. Breathe this way for several minutes.

- As you breathe, your imagination flashes an image that represents this problem. Taking whatever time you need, receive what comes first as fully as you can.

- As you sense this image, notice its details.

- Magically, this image becomes a movie that plays out *the perfect answer* to this problem. Take some time to sense it.

- After the movie has reached a resolution, rewind it, jump into it, and live it. Notice how this feels.

- When you are ready, record or share your experience, noticing how it feels.

OUT-OF-THE-BOX INVENTIONS

- Take whatever time you need to settle into a relaxed, closed-eyes state, as your body moves into deeper and deeper relaxation.

- As you settle into this more relaxed state, your imagination puts a magical hat on your head that reminds you of childlike joy. Notice this hat and how it looks and feels.

- As you feel the immense power of your new hat, a magnificently wrapped present drops from the sky right in front of you! It is wrapped beautifully in exactly a way that appeals to you. Notice the colors, textures, and designs, including the tag that says, "Love from Your Soul."

- When you are ready, unwrap this magical gift.

- Feel the texture and hear the sound of colorful tissue paper in the box, as you find an object.

- Picking up the object, feel it in your hands and notice the specifics of its weight, colors, function. Easily sense this invention and how it's perfect for you.

- Notice how it feels to hold this object, dialogue with it, and sense answers to your questions.

- When you are ready, record what you've learned and share it with others, noticing how it feels.

QUESTIONS & ANSWERS ABOUT RIM

Regenerating Images in Memory

What Is RIM®?

RIM® or *"Regenerating Images in Memory"* is a client-generated, body-centered process that activates one's native emotional system to stimulate dramatic emotional and physical healing, greater insight, creativity, and effective problem-solving. Dr. Deborah Sandella originated it more than twenty years ago. Initially, she synthesized aspects of Ericksonian hypnosis, Interactive Guided Imagery, and an early form of somatic sensing. Since that time, RIM has evolved with its own unique skills and philosophy. Most techniques use willpower to reframe thoughts. In contrast, RIM gives form to emotions so they can be transformed visibly at a visceral or gut level. When source events are uncovered and regenerated, empowered thoughts, feelings, and behaviors generate automatically without conscious reframing.

How Does It Work?

RIM unravels painful emotion by using imagination to 1) identify and redo the source of emotional blocks, 2) materialize emotional resources, and 3) surface creative/intuitive answers. The process can be self-applied or facilitated by others.

What Is RIM's Philosophy?

The foundational philosophy of RIM is that each of us is born whole. Traumatic life experiences create memory that layers on top of our whole nature. We sometimes confuse the residue of these experiences with who we are, but RIM helps us dissolve and redo painful feelings and memories, similar to wiping layers of dust from the living room furniture, so that our natural brilliance and liveliness shine through. Given this philosophy, the process is client-generated and organic. RIM facilitators trust the client's emotional operating system and apply twenty-three skills to activate and program it. Thus, clients effortlessly uproot an issue at the gut level, creating automatic emotional and behavioral transformation.

Can RIM Be Used with Groups?

Yes, the process can be used with groups.

Can RIM Be Done over the Phone and via Skype?

Yes, it can be done over the phone and with Skype because RIM is not based in the facilitator-client relationship. Rather, the relationship fostered is between the client and him/herself.

How Long Are Facilitated Sessions?

RIM activities can be as brief as ten to fifteen minutes, while facilitated sessions range from one to two hours.

How Many RIM Sessions Are Necessary?

Each RIM activity/session accomplishes a specific piece of work that produces positive results. Some people gain what they need in one session, and others engage in a series of sessions to address a range of issues. Three to five sessions are common. Similar to findings with other techniques such as neurofeedback, a deficit of serotonin in the body (biochemical depression) can make it difficult for session benefits to sustain. For these few people, good results are best achieved by increasing their level of serotonin in addition to session(s).

Has RIM Been Researched?

Yes. Dr. Audrey Boxwell found that RIM significantly decreases the hallmark symptoms of stress-related illness and significantly increases one's quality of life.[1]

Furthermore, a recent survey of Dr. Deb's clients showed a statistically significantly increase in the frequency of each of the following behaviors/feelings, regardless of the number of RIM sessions* or the length of time since the last session/s:[†]

1. I own up to my mistakes and shortcomings, even when I am embarrassed.

2. I am willing to try new things, even when I am uncomfortable or scared.

3. I take responsibility for my feelings rather than blaming others.

4. I meet my financial goals.

5. I am happy with my career growth.

6. I meet my recreational time and fun time goals.

7. I meet my physical fitness and health goals.

8. I enjoy most of the relationships with my family and friends.

9. I live free of shame.

10. I am self-aware.

11. I believe I am supported by life.

(Statistician and Researcher: Heather Blizzard, University of Denver doctoral candidate)

*There was improvement in each area regardless of the number of sessions.

†Even three years after their RIM session, clients reported improvement.

Further research is planned, and the RIM Institute welcomes research partners.

Are There Contraindications for RIM?

RIM is contraindicated for people who have a mental illness, especially if their condition interrupts their ability to discern reality, such as psychosis, schizophrenia, manic depression, and/or paranoia.

How Do I Become a RIM Facilitator?

There are several levels of RIM training. Because RIM is a specific transformational technique, not therapy, a counseling degree is not required.

Go to *www.RIMinstitute.com* and click on the RIM Institute page for details. The RIM process is commonly used as an effective tool to maximize client results in life coaching, psychotherapy, corporate consulting, nursing, workshop facilitating, education, integrative medicine, and numerous other professions. Certified RIM facilitators also create stand-alone practices.

How Do I Find a RIM Facilitator?

Go to *www.RIMinstitute.com* and click on the RIM Institute page, where there's a sidebar link to the Directory of Certified RIM Facilitators, or call toll-free at 888-788-0800.

Is Dr. Deb Available for Speaking and Workshops?

Yes, she offers interactive and entertaining keynotes and workshops where the audience gets to witness and experience their inherent powers of imagination and emotion. She also offers four-day retreats for groups of ten people interested in quantum-level results in addition to the RIM facilitator training programs. Her organizational communication background makes her an excellent choice for team-building sessions for businesses small and large. Go to *www.RIMinstitute.com* or *www.GoodbyeHurtandPain. com* for more information.

ACKNOWLEDGMENTS

As I sense all the people and experiences that have contributed to my journey through this book, I realize: they're everywhere . . . they're everywhere! I'm deeply grateful to Jack Canfield, Patty Aubrey, Russ Kamalski, Kathleen Seeley and senior staff, Jesse Ianniello, Andrea Haefele-Ventim, Alice Refauvelet, Lisa Williams, and Kajsa Garrett, for being my beautiful work family. And to Inga Canfield for discovering me. Eleven years ago I heard in meditation: *"You're supposed to go to Jack Canfield's seminar."* When I asked, *"Why?"* The answer was, *"You'll find out."* Yes, I have found a work family whom I love dearly.

Thanks to my editor Caroline Pincus, who has been an enthusiastic and beneficial force on this project. Sharing a passion for the subject, she's been an empowering partner. Also, many thanks to editor Greg Brandenburgh, production editor Jane Hagaman, cover artist Jim Warner, and marketers Eryn Carter and Bonni Hamilton for their invaluable support in putting it all together. And I'm grateful to my agent Jeff Herman, who believed in this book and my writing. He graciously walked me through doubt and helped find the right words. Thanks to Steve Harrison, who connected me with Jeff. Additional gratitude for a great job by Mark Gelotte for graphically shaping emotion into creative form; his illustrations speak the language of the unconscious beautifully, and his willingness to help me personalize the cover image was invaluable.

Other partners include all those who have answered the call to pioneer RIM. I am humbled by their service and commitment to this newly traveled path. Junia Imel, Jaroslav Prusa, Madelaine Osborne, Teresa Huggins, Lynn Hellerstein—you were the trailblazers, and I thank you. I am grateful for the RIM facilitators past, present, and future—you are the next generation—Michael Kline, Emily Alberts, Colleen Sweeney, Lotte Vesterli, Kenneth Cole, Anita Sanchez, Andrea Kneier, Sue Lewis, Kathy Sparrow, Audrey Boxwell, MaryAnn McDonald, Chanda Carlson, Steve Torneten, Stephanie Ecke, Lili Boggess, Denisa Prusova, Michelle Kaplan, Joan Newsom, plus too many to name. I'm so happy to walk with all of you as we go beyond the RIM to awaken all of us to unrealized power and brilliance.

Thank you to all the clients who bravely ventured into their rawest feelings. I am honored to have shared your deeply intimate experiences. You inspire me.

To all my teachers throughout the years, I'm deeply appreciative of your knowledge and wisdom, including Jack Canfield, Stephen Gilligan, David Bresler, Martin Rossman, Harville Hendricks, Maya Kollman, Roger Teal, Marjorie Staum, Patty Lucas, Carl Larson, Alton Barbour, Dort Gregg, Faye Spring, Betsy Wiersma, Cynthia James, and Cathy and Gary Hawk.

How blessed I am to have been born into a playful and loving family. I send immense gratitude to my dad watching from above and my mom, who brought me into a lineage of ageless women. To my sister Dee, brother Gregg, and all their children, thanks for wonderful memories that keep on coming and bringing me joy.

To my adult children Walker and Elena: You are exquisite. How did I get so lucky? I love you always and forever. You inspire me no matter what I'm doing. And Jess, how wonderful to have you join our family . . . Walker chose perfectly!

To Dick Fullerton: What a journey it has been through all these years of growing up, older and kinder together. You are my greatest teacher and supporter. How would I live without you . . . and your editing? I love you!

I'm infinitely grateful to be with every one of you on this curious adventure of life! Salud!

ENDNOTES

INTRODUCTION

1   Excerpt from Deb Sandella, "Beyond the RIM of Imagination," *Science of Mind*, 86, no. 9 (September 2013): 70–76.

2   Sources: Susan Everson-Rose, PhD, MPH, associate professor, medicine, University of Minnesota, Minneapolis; Jeffrey Borenstein, MD, president and CEO, Brain & Behavior Research Foundation, New York; Richard Libman, MD, chief, vascular neurology, North Shore-LIJ Health System, Manhasset, New York, *Stroke* online (August 2014).

3   Amit Shah, MD, assistant professor, epidemiology, Rollins School of Public Health, Emory University, Atlanta; Michael W. O'Hara, PhD, professor, psychology, University of Iowa, Iowa City, Iowa, *Journal of the American Heart Association* online (June 18, 2014).

4   *www.stress.org*.

5   Madhu Kalia, "Assessing the Economic Impact of Stress— The Modern Day Hidden Epidemic," *Metabolism, Clinical and Experimental*, 51, issue 6, part B (June 2002): 49–53.

6   Daniel Goleman, *Emotional Intelligence: Why It Can Matter More than IQ* (New York: Bantam Books, 1995), 12.

7   Fred Howard, *Wilbur and Orville: A Biography of the Wright Brothers* (Mineola, NY: Dover Publications, 1998), 33.

STEP ONE: FLOW & GO

1   *dictionary.com:* word origin of "emotion."

2   Hildy S. Ross, (University of Waterloo, Ontario, Canada), "The Influence of Novelty and Complexity on Exploratory Behavior in 12-Month-Old Infants," *Journal of Experimental Child Psychology* 17, issue 3, (1974): 436–51.

3   A.D. (Bud) Craig, "Interoception and Emotion: A Neuro-anatomical Perspective," *Handbook of Emotions* (New York: Guilford Press, 2008): 272–88.

4   Giovanni Manobianca, MD, et al., "Gross Domestic Product and Health Expenditure Associated with Incidence, 30-Day Fatality, and Age at Stroke Onset: A Systematic Review," *Stroke,* 43 (2012), 170–77.

5   Aron Wolfe Siegman (University of Maryland Baltimore County) and Timothy W. Smith (University of Utah), eds., *Anger, Hostility, and the Heart,* Psychology Press, (1993).

6   Johannes Eichstaedt (Psychology Dept., University of Pennsylvania) et al., *Psychological Science* (January 20, 2015), 0956797614557867 online Sage Journals.

7   Sharon Jayson, "Americans Seem Angry a Lot, but It's All in the Management," *USA Today* (November 18, 2009).

8   Siegman and Smith, *Anger, Hostility, and the Heart,* xiv.

9   Dictionary: Rorschach test, known as the Rorschach inkblot test, the Rorschach technique, or simply the inkblot test, is a psychological test in which subjects' perceptions of inkblots are recorded and then analyzed using psychological interpretation, complex algorithms, or both. The test is named after its creator, Swiss psychologist Hermann Rorschach.

10 Deborah Sandella, *Releasing the Inner Magician* (Denver, CO: The Inner Magician Series, original 2002, revised ed. 2010).

11 Based on Gendlin's focusing technique and expanded to reflect RIM process. Eugene Gendlin, *Focusing*. (New York: Bantam Books, 2007, originally Everest House, 1978).

STEP TWO: SEE & FREE

1   Audrey Boxwell and David Eichler, "The Efficacy of Guided Imagery/Visualization & Journaling in Patients with Irritable Bowel Syndrome," *Subtle Energies & Energy Medicine* 16, no. 2 (2006): 21–24.

2   Richard Fisher, *New Scientist*, 214, issue 2869 (2012): 34–37.

3   Benjamin Baird, et al., *Psychological Science* 23, no. 10 (October 2012): 1117–22.

4   Shelley Carson, *Journal of Personality and Social Psychology* 85 (2003): 49.

5   John Kounios and Mark Beeman, "The Aha! Moment: The Cognitive Neuroscience of Insight," *Current Directions in Psychological Science* 18 (2009): 210.

6   Malia Mason, *Science* 315, no. 5810 (2007): 393–95.

7   K. Christof, et al., "Experience Sampling during fMRI Reveals Default Network and Executive System Contributions to Mind Wandering," *Proceedings of the National Academy of Sciences* 106(21): 8719–24.

8   Rosalind Cartwright, *The Twenty-Four Hour Mind* (New York: Oxford University Press, 2010): 54.

9   Cartwright, *The Twenty-Four Hour Mind*, 55.

10 Cartwright, *The Twenty-Four Hour Mind*, 56.

11 G. W. Domhoff and K. R. Fox, "Dreaming and the Default Network: A Review, Synthesis, and Counterintuitive Research Proposal," *Consciousness and Cognition* 33 (2015): 342–53.

12 E. Klinger, *Daydreaming: Using Waking Fantasy and Imagery for Self-Knowledge and Creativity* (Los Angeles: Tarcher, 1990): 16, 64.

13 Boxwell and Eichler, "The Efficacy of Guided Imagery/Visualization & Journaling in Patients with Irritable Bowel Syndrome."

STEP THREE: UPSTICK & UP-WICK

1   Rick Hanson, PhD with Richard Mendius, MD, *Buddha's Brain: The Practical Neuroscience of Happiness, Love, and Wisdom* (Oakland, CA: New Harbinger Publications, Inc., 2009).

2   Bessel Van der Kolk, MD, *The Body Keeps the Score* (New York: Viking, c. 2014), 24–25.

3   Alison Holman, Dana Rose Garfin, and Roxane Cohen Silver, "Media's Role in Broadcasting Acute Stress Following the Boston Marathon Bombings," edited by Shelley E. Taylor, Proceedings of the National Academy of Sciences of the United States of America (PNAS) (University of California, Los Angeles, November 14, 2013).

4   G. Rizzolatti and L. Craighero, "The Mirror-Neuron System," *Annual Review of Neuroscience* 27 (2004): 169–92.

5   *dictionary.com:* "word origin" section.

6   Sandella, *Releasing the Inner Magician.*

7   *dictionary.com:* "com" and "passion."

8   Van der Kolk, *The Body Keeps the Score.*

9   Timothy Wilson, et al., "Just Think: The Challenges of the Disengaged Mind," *Science* 4 (July 2014): 75–77.

10 Inspired by a Doreen Virtue meditation.

11 Brené Brown, *The Gifts of Imperfection* (Center City, MN: Hazelden Publishing and Education, 2010).

12 Boxwell, and Eichler, "The Efficacy of Guided Imagery/Visualization & Journaling in Patients with Irritable Bowel Syndrome."

STEP FOUR: ME & THEE

1 *dictionary.com.*

2 *dictionary.com:* synonyms of the word "whole."

3 S. L. Master, et al., "A Picture's Worth: Partner Photographs Reduce Experimentally Induced Pain," *Psychological Science* 20 (2009): 1316–18.

4 Wolfgang Taube, et al., "Brain Activity during Observation and Motor Imagery of Different Balance Tasks: An fMRI Study," *Cortex* 64 (March 2015): 102–14.

5 Van der Kolk, *The Body Keeps the Score.*

6 Van der Kolk, *The Body Keeps the Score.*

STEP FIVE: REPEL & ATTRACT

1 Candance Pert, *Molecules of Emotion: Why You Feel the Way You Feel* (New York: Simon and Schuster Touchstone, February 1997).

2 Robert Sapolsky, *Why Zebras Don't Get Ulcers: The Acclaimed Guide to Stress, Stress-Related Diseases, and Coping* (New York: Henry Holt and Company, 2004).

3 V. Felitti, et al., "Relationship of Childhood Abuse and Household Dysfunction to Many of the Leading Causes of Death in Adults: The Adverse Childhood Experiences (ACE) Study," *American Journal of Preventive Medicine* 14, no. 4 (1998): 245–58.

4 Bruce Ecker, Robin Ticic, and Laurel Hulley, *Unlocking the Emotional Brain* (New York: Routledge, Taylor & Francis Group, 2012), 34.

5   Pat Ogden, Keguni Minton, and Clare Pain, *Trauma and the Body* (New York: W. W. Norton & Company, 2006).

6   Ecker, Ticic, and Hulley, Laurel, *Unlocking the Emotional Brain, 4.*

STEP SIX: SQUEEZE & BREEZE

1   *dictionary.com:* word origin.

2   *dictionary.com:* antonyms.

3   Stephen Bayley, *Ugly: The Aesthetics of Everything* (New York: Overlook Hardcover, 2013).

STEP SEVEN: REDO & RENEW

1   Felitti, et al., "Relationship of Childhood Abuse and Household Dysfunction to Many of the Leading Causes of Death in Adults: The Adverse Childhood Experiences (ACE) Study," 245–58.

2   Jennifer M. Talarico and David C. Rubin, "Confidence, not Consistency, Characterizes Flashbulb Memories," *Psychological Science* 14.5 (2003): 455–61.

3   Julian Barnes, *Nothing to Be Frightened Of* (New York: Knopf eBook, 2008).

4   Van der Kolk, *The Body Keeps the Score*, 217.

5   Karim Nader, Glenn Schafe, and Joseph Le Doux, "Fear Memories Require Protein Synthesis in the Amygdala for Reconsolidating after Retrieval," *Nature* 406 (August 2000), 722–26.

6   Daniel Schacter, *Searching for Memory* (New York: Basic Books, A Member of Perseus Books, 1996).

7 Phone and Skype sessions, *www.RIMinstitute.com,* or toll-free 888-788-0800.

8 RIM is not intended for people with mental illness that interferes with reality testing, such as: psychosis, schizophrenia, manic depression, and paranoid delusions.

9 Brian G. Dias and Kerry J. Ressler, "Parental Olfactory Experience Influences Behavior and Neural Structure in Subsequent Generations," *Nature Neuroscience* 17 (2014): 89–96.

10 R. Yehuda, et al., *American Journal of Psychiatry* 171(8) (August 2014): 872–80, doi: 10.1176/appi.ajp.2014.13121571. Influences of maternal and paternal PTSD on epigenetic regulation of the glucocorticoid receptor gene in Holocaust survivor offspring.

11 Quote from Smucker, Mervin, and Dancu, Constance, *Cognitive-Behavioral Treatment for Adult Survivors of Childhood Trauma: Imagery Rescripting and Reprocessing* (Langham, MD: Rowman & Littlefield, 2005; originally UK: Jason Aronson, 1999), 23. Citation: C. Jung, translated by R. F. C. Hull, *The Portable Jung* (New York: Penguin, 1971).

12 Jack Canfield, and Janet Switzer, *The Success Principles*, 10th anniversary edition (New York: William Morrow, 2015): 107–22.

13 Taube, et al., "Brain Activity during Observation and Motor Imagery of Different Balance Tasks: An fMRI Study."

14 J. B. Moseley, et al., "A Controlled Trial of Arthroscopic Surgery for Osteoarthritis of the Knee," *New England Journal of Medicine* 347(2) (July 2002): 81–88.

15 S. M. Schafer, L. Colloca, and T. D. Wager, "Conditioned Placebo Analgesia Persists When Subjects Know They Are Receiving a Placebo," *Journal of Pain* 16(5) (May 2015): 412–20.

BRINGING IT ALL TOGETHER

1 Van der Kolk, *The Body Keeps the Score.*

2 Jack Canfield and David Andrews, *The 30-Day Sobriety Solution* (New York: Atria Books, 2016).

3 Joe Dispenza, *You Are the Placebo: Making Your Mind Matter* (New York: Hay House, Inc., 2014): 152.

4 John Kounios and Mark Beeman, "The Aha! Moment: The Cognitive Neuroscience of Insight," *Current Directions in Psychological Science* 18 (2009): 210.

5 Van der Kolk, *The Body Keeps the Score,* 95–96.

6 Richard P. Chi, Allan W. Snyder, and Dorothy Bishop, "Facilitate Insight by Non-Invasive Brain Stimulation," *PLOS One* 6, no. 2 (2011).

7 The brain's neurology is not so black and white, yet the general idea of left and right brain qualities is a simplification that helps us understand the value of both ways of processing information.

8 A. Olincy, et al., "Proof-of-Concept Trial of an $\alpha 7$ Nicotinic Agonist in Schizophrenia," *Archives of General Psychiatry* 63(6) (2006): 630–38.

9 Jill Bolte Taylor, *My Stroke of Insight* (New York: Viking, 2006).

10 E. Kross, et al., "Social Rejection Shares Somatosensory Representations with Physical Pain," *Proceedings of the National Academy of Sciences* 108 (2011): 6270–75.

11 N. I. Eisenberger, "Broken Hearts and Broken Bones: A Neural Perspective on the Similarities between Social and Physical Pain," *Current Directions in Psychological Science* 21 (2012): 42–47.

12 C. N. DeWall, et al., "Tylenol Reduces Social Pain: Behavioral and Neural Evidence," *Psychological Science* 21 (2010): 931–37.

13 John Arden, *The Brain Bible* (Boston: McGraw Hill Education, 2014).

14 *dictionary.com:* based on Random House Dictionary, 2015.

15 Stephen W. Porges, *The Polyvagal Theory: Neurophysiological Foundations of Emotions, Attachment, Communication and Self-Regulation* (New York: W. W. Norton and Co., 2011).

16 P. Ekman, *Emotions Revealed: Recognizing Faces and Feelings to Improve Communication and Emotional Life* (New York: Macmillan, 2007).

SIMPLE AND SPEEDY RIM TOOLS FOR DAILY LIFE

1 RIM-Enhanced Milton Erickson Hypnosis Activity.

QUESTIONS & ANSWERS ABOUT RIM

1 Boxwell and Eichler, "The Efficacy of Guided Imagery/ Visualization & Journaling in Patients with Irritable Bowel Syndrome."

INDEX

ABOUT THE AUTHOR

Deborah Sandella lives in Colorado with her husband. She enjoys hiking the trails and camping under 14,000 foot peaks (climbing a couple), and can't imagine not having 300 days of sunshine. Deb loves personal and professional adventure and pushing the limits. Early in her career, she developed an intensive mental health program that decreased hospital stays from three weeks to three days and kept patients connected with their families. Over the last twenty years, she's discovered how to activate one's emotional operating system for quicker and more effective ways to have health, love and success. She calls it the RIM Method (Regenerating Images in Memory) and has founded the RIM Institute where others learn to apply the technique with themselves and their clients to improve personal and professional success.

TO OUR READERS

Conari Press, an imprint of Red Wheel/Weiser, publishes books on topics ranging from spirituality, personal growth, and relationships to women's issues, parenting, and social issues. Our mission is to publish quality books that will make a difference in people's lives—how we feel about ourselves and how we relate to one another. We value integrity, compassion, and receptivity, both in the books we publish and in the way we do business.

Our readers are our most important resource, and we appreciate your input, suggestions, and ideas about what you would like to see published.

Visit our website at *www.redwheelweiser.com* to learn about our upcoming books and free downloads, and be sure to go to *www.redwheelweiser.com/newsletter* to sign up for newsletters and exclusive offers.

You can also contact us at *info@rwwbooks.com*.

Conari Press
an imprint of Red Wheel/Weiser, LLC
65 Parker Street, Suite 7
Newburyport, MA 01950
www.redwheelweiser.com